D0000155

MENTAL GAME PLAN:

Getting psyched for sport

Stephen J. Bull, PhD.
John G. Albinson, PhD.
Christopher J. Shambrook, PhD.

© 1996

First published in 1996 by
Sports Dynamics
Reprinted in 1997 and 1999.

Available in the UK and Europe from:-

Sports Dynamics
20, Greenway Lane
CHELTENHAM,
GL52 6LB, UK

Tel/Fax: 01242 515 383

Email: sports.dynamics@virgin.net

Available in North America from:-

Fitness Information Technology,
PO Box 4425
University Avenue,
Morgantown
WV 26504-4425,
USA

Tel/Fax: +304-599-3482.

A catalogue record for this book
is available from the British Library.

ISBN 0 9519543 2 6

Page design, layout and typesetting by Myrene McFee.
Cover layout by KRS Design.

Printed and bound by
Fotodirect Ltd, Brighton, UK

Tottenham Hotspur used it.
Monica Seles wouldn't be playing
without it.
Even England rugby players
believe in it....

Sport psychology
is as much the key to success
today as any training
or coaching.

John Roberts
in *The Independent Newspaper*, 1995

Contents

About the authors

Dr Stephen J. Bull

Steve Bull is a writer and consultant in sport psychology. He has made invited presentations and travelled with performers in over 10 different countries around the world and has published 5 books in the area. He has worked with the 1994 and 2000 Great Britain Olympic teams; the England Men's and Women's Cricket Teams; the British Ski Team; British Equestrian Teams and with individuals in Premiership Football and Rugby, the professional tennis circuit, the European PGA Golf Tour and professional county cricket. He also applies his work in the business world where he has consulted with a number of well known companies. Steve played county rugby at Under 23 and Senior Levels, county cricket and athletics at schoolboy level and has completed three marathons. He currently enjoys competitive squash and golf.

Dr John G. Albinson

John Albinson is an Associate Professor in sport psychology at Queen's University in Canada. He has been consulting with athletes and teams for twenty five years and has worked with performers at all levels. John has been President of the Canadian Society for Psychomotor Learning and Sport Psychology and Chair of the Sport Science and Medical Committee of a National Governing Body. He worked as a consultant at the 1984 Olympic Games in Los Angeles. Recreationally, John enjoys curling, hiking and various outdoor pursuits.

Dr Christopher J. Shambrook

Chris Shambrook is currently sport psychologist to the Great Britain Rowing Team, and has been working with them for the past three years in the build up to the Sydney Olympic Games. He has attended three World Championships and numerous training camps. In addition to work in rowing, Chris has provided sport psychology services in Premier Football, Premier Rugby, County Cricket, and with many other national and international performers. He has presented his research work at national and international conferences, and has published in practical and academic outlets. When possible Chris enjoys attempting to beat Steve at golf, and works out regularly to keep fit.

Chapter 1
Sport psychology: The mental toughness plan

Sport is only partly about ability, talent, accuracy, skill: all those lovely things. To think otherwise is to be taken in by sport's great illusion. But talent is not enough in any sport. For it is not superior ability that separates champions from contenders. It is superior nerve. It is the ability to respond to a clutch situation by playing your best.

The classic example is the two-foot putt. Even the non-golfer can knock in two-foot putts. But could we do it for a bet of a million pounds? Or when the Ryder Cup depends on it? Most of us could walk along the kerb without a hint of concern about falling into the gutter. But supposing the kerb was 3,000 feet off the ground? Not so easy. And that is what a clutch situation means.

Simon Barnes wrote these words in *The Times Newspaper* following Rob Andrew's famous drop-kick in the quarter final of the Rugby World Cup in 1995 between England and Australia.

More and more articles are beginning to appear in the popular press which address the psychology of sports performance. Coaches, managers, and athletes themselves frequently refer to the importance of the mental side of competition. Mental toughness is a term commonly used. Athletes, coaches and managers agree that this is an extremely important attribute to possess if a top level performance is desired. Like Simon Barnes, many athletes go so far as to suggest that, on the day of competition, it is this mental toughness which is the deciding factor. This, they claim, is the case because at the highest levels in modern sport there is so little to separate performers in technical competence or physical fitness.

Mental toughness is also an important element in training. In order to reach high levels of performance, athletes must endure long hours of strenuous training regimes which can be boring and tiring. Athletes must cope with bad luck, injuries and various uncontrollable factors which will influence the smooth running of their training programmes. Mental toughness will assist in coping with these setbacks as well as enduring the pressures of intensive training workloads.

Athletes in the public eye must also deal with media interest and the invasion of privacy. Mental toughness will assist the athlete in coping with these inconvenient, and often upsetting, intrusions which have significantly affected many performers in the past.

> **It is mental power that separates the exceptional from the very good. When they line up for the 100 metre sprint in Barcelona there will be nothing to choose between them, talent for talent, training for training. What separates them is what goes on behind the eyes.**
>
> *Frank Dick,*
> *former coach to the*
> *Great Britain track*
> *and field team*

What is this thing called mental toughness?

And what exactly can we do to develop it? This is what this book is about. It is a down to earth approach to applying sport psychology principles and will teach you how you can utilise a range of different mental training techniques which have been tried and tested by world class sports performers.

Most athletes, if given enough time and competitive opportunities, will use and practise mental skills on their own because they find that by doing so their performances are much more consistent. However, most athletes do not have the luxury of unlimited time and competitive opportunities. Many potentially outstanding athletes stop competing before they get near their potential because they could not perform at the highest levels as a result of poor mental skills and lack of mental toughness. Other athletes could achieve even higher levels of performance if they were better able to use mental skills effectively. Most international performers indicate that they do, in fact, use specific mental skills but they had to learn them through trial and error. Many express the feeling that they could have been performing at even higher levels earlier in their careers if they had been taught the skills rather than having to learn them the hard way.

> **I think the biggest problem facing athletes today is the lack of good mental preparation.**
>
> *Sylvie Bernier,*
> *Olympic Diving*
> *Gold Medalist*

The mental skills which are important in the performance of sport skills are those which enable the athlete to reach a state of mind which will prevent negative, and distracting, thoughts interfering with physical performance. If you execute a sport skill successfully once (such as a superb golf shot down the middle of the fairway), then you have the physical capability to achieve that successful execution every time you try. But you don't — because the mind interferes and spoils the physical coordination as opposed to enhancing it. The mental skills to which we are referring are not new. Many of them have been used for centuries. An ancient book which describes the training programme for the Samurai warriors of Japan devoted half of the text to the mental preparation of these superior athlete warriors. The former Eastern bloc nations were utilising the services of sport psychology in the early 1960s. However, it has only been comparatively recently that Western countries have begun to fully appreciate the significant role that serious mental skills training can play in the performance of a sports competitor. For example, it was not until the Barcelona Olympic Games of 1992 that Great Britain had a notable presence of sport psychologists to assist in athlete preparation. Indeed, the British Olympic Association now has a group of experienced sport psychologists who meet regularly to discuss the best ways of delivering mental training to athletes in the various Olympic sports. Similar groups exist in the USA, Canada, Australia and many other countries.

However, the systematic development of mental training techniques should not wait until an athlete is at an elite level such as being a member of a national squad. These skills should be taught to younger athletes in the same manner that physical and technical skills are taught. If this happens, the young athletes can use the skills as they develop and improve. This will enhance their rate of progress as the trial and error process is bypassed. The athletes will build up an armoury of mental skills which can be deployed at appropriate times during training, preparation and competition.

The process of developing the mental skills of young athletes is the same as the process for developing technical skills. In technical development, everyone is shown the most efficient style of performing a particular skill and is advised to use it. As the athlete improves, this classic style is adapted to the particular body type, strength, limb length and personality of the specific athlete. In the beginning, the skills are *taught*. Then, the *coaching* process moulds the style to fit the needs of the athlete in order to produce the best possible performance.

This process can also be followed in the development of mental skills. The skills are initially taught, and then moulded to fit the individual athlete and facilitate optimum performance. The sooner the athlete learns to use mental skills training, the sooner certain performance obstacles can be tackled — such as frustration with inconsistent performances; poor performance due to over-anxiety; distraction due to errors; and lack of confidence or positive attitude.

In our work as sport psychology consultants, we usually begin a programme of mental skills training by introducing athletes to ways in which they can facilitate the development of mental toughness.

In our experience of working with many world class performers, we have found that mentally tough athletes possess a number of related attributes — each of which is an element of the overall mental toughness quality.

Mental toughness attributes

● 1 *Strong desire to succeed*

World champions often talk about how very clearly they had targeted their ultimate achievement long before it was achieved. Their training programmes had a real sense of purpose. Their sporting career had an obvious direction. And, they really wanted to reach their potential. Athletes at all levels can learn from this approach. They should ask themselves questions such as does my training programme have a real sense of purpose? Do I know where I'm going and how I'm going to get there? How badly do I want to improve and achieve in my sport? Am I prepared to make the necessary sacrifices in order to progress?

Most top sports performers have detailed goal setting

The greatest professional quality is not money, but attitude.

John Monie,
highly
successful
Australian rugby
league coach

programmes which have been established in consultation with a coach. Each training session has a specific purpose and is viewed as a small step towards a longer term goal. They do not bumble through training sessions in a mediocre fashion. They are focused, committed and dedicated to achievement. They take personal responsibility in delivering excellence (a useful acronym for motivation sessions — P.R.I.D.E). And they are not put off by setbacks and lack of progress.

So, why not begin by questioning your own commitment and desire? How badly do you really want to succeed? Do you have a goal programme which forms a structured part of your overall training regime? Are you prepared to make the necessary sacrifices to get where you want to be?

● 2   *Stay positive in the face of challenge and pressure*

An integral part of competitive sport is challenge and pressure. If athletes cannot cope with this they are not mentally tough. Jim Loehr (who has worked with top tennis players at the Bollettieri academy in Florida) talks about competition as a continuous presentation of problems. He claims that it is your emotional response to problems which brings either success or failure as a competitor. Loehr warns against entering the competitive arena expecting things to run smoothly — most of the time they won't and you must be able to deal with this in a confident and controlled manner.

Loehr is a specialist in tennis psychology and provides a good example of mental toughness in a tennis player. It concerns a cheating opponent who continually makes bad line calls. He advises that when a player is convinced that the opponent is cheating and

> If you haven't had the results you want, you just have to learn from it, rebuild and regroup.
>
> **Nick Faldo**, *champion golfer speaking after a bad run of tournaments in 1995*

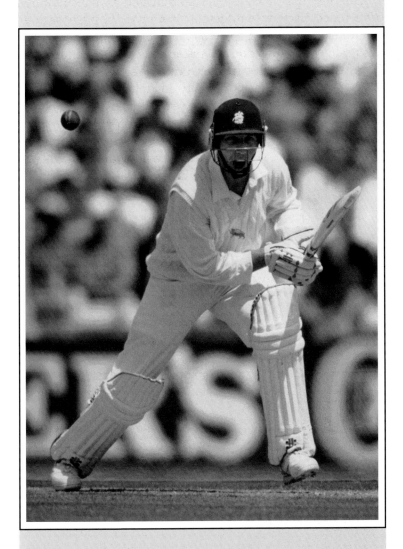

"Just because you have played badly doesn't mean you should accept defeat."

Michael Atherton, Captain of the England Cricket Team, after batting for almost 11 hours to save the second Test against South Africa in 1995

making bad line calls, then it is important to dig in and get challenged. He says that the player should not make excuses or complain but rather refuse to be beaten by someone who is deliberately making bad calls. This is mental toughness and it is this attitude which so many sports performers need to work on. All sports have their potential versions of Loehr's line calling scenario. Athletes should ask themselves how good they are at dealing with situations such as this.

The famous motor racing driver Nigel Mansell provides a good example of dealing with bad luck and adversity. Terence O'Rorke describes Mansell in the following way:

> *"It is the sign of a true sporting champion when you can come back from the pits of despair.....in Nigel Mansell, Britain has a sportsman of rare determination. A sportsman who has suffered more setbacks than most, but has still managed to pull through because of his exceptional self-belief. By winning the 1992/93 Formula One Driver's World Championship, Mansell has given us a unique insight into how to turn adversity into advantage; he has learned from every moment of failure and taken stock of every piece of bad luck. Each experience has helped to make him even more dogged in his pursuit of sporting excellence.... Nigel Mansell's bad luck is legendary."*

So, how good are you at staying positive under pressure? Assess your sport-related thinking. Do you engage in pressure-producing thinking or are your thoughts more positive? Do you love the challenge of tough competition? How well do you cope with bad luck, hassles and adversity?

● 3   Control the controllables

Sport psychologists often talk about the importance of controlling the controllables. It is a waste of valuable mental energy to worry about, or get angry about uncontrollable factors such as poor weather, inferior equipment or the experience of the opposition. We advise athletes to focus on things they can do something about. This means putting effort into ensuring your technical, physical and mental preparation is the best it can possibly be on competition day. Organise your training

Graham Bell, as a British skier lacking large sponsorship and hence backup support, has had to take personal responsibility for much of his equipment preparation. This has sometimes meant missing fitness sessions to prepare his skis. On these occasions he must concentrate on "controlling the controllables".

programme and stick to it. Devote time to mental training techniques. Make sure your equipment is well prepared and that you have planned for unexpected eventualities. Discuss performance issues with your coach and make sure you enter the competitive arena feeling, and thinking, positive. If you do these things well, you've done as much as you can. Then, go out and enjoy it!

So, how good are you at staying positive when things go wrong? Do you tend to worry about uncontrollable factors? Do you lose confidence when luck is not on your side?

● 4   High commitment with a balanced attitude

Top sports performers get there through a long process of hard work. The former World Champion skier, Kate Pace, connected a card to the handlebars of the bicycle she used for stamina training. Written on this card were the words "If you don't train hard today — someone else will." To sustain this attitude week after week requires mental toughness. Along the way sacrifices are necessary which can present strains in other areas of life — particularly family, career and social life. To cope with this requires mental toughness. So, the following questions are worth considering.

"To what extent am I prepared to make the necessary sacrifices in order to succeed in my sport?"

"Do I give 100% in training as well as competition — even if things aren't going so well?"

"Am I prepared to put in extra time on physical and mental preparation?"

"Can I take responsibility for my own development and dedicate myself fully to my training and competition programme?"

"Just how committed am I?"

I'm not involved in tennis, I am committed. Do you know the difference between involvement and commitment?

Martina Navratilova, former tennis champion

However, maintaining a balanced outlook is crucial in the long term. Sport should not consume your life to the point where everything else loses meaning. Family, friends and other interests can be the best antidotes for coping with sporting disappointments. So, it's important to enjoy competition for its own sake, rather than on the basis of whether you win or lose. Even if

> **You've got to have fun and laugh a lot.**
>
> *Kirsten Barnes,*
> *Canadian rower and double Olympic Gold Medalist*

you do lose, there's usually another opportunity in the future. Take time out from your sporting obsession from time to time and enjoy other things. You'll find that you return refreshed and ready to fight again. Don't mope and moan for long periods after disappointing performances. You'll simply bring yourself further down. Count your blessings, pick up the pieces and look forward to competing next time. Sport should be fun and we feel that enjoyment is a big part of athletic mental toughness.

● 5   High level of self-belief

Mentally tough athletes have a real sense of self-belief. They are extremely confident and believe that they have the capacity to perform well under the most challenging situations. When things start to go wrong, they have the ability to refocus, and come back strong. They never give up even when it looks like it's all over. Tennis players talk about the tendency of certain players to "tank". This means they throw the match away when things aren't going so well by hitting the ball as hard as possible with a "what the heck" attitude. A mentally tough performer would not do this under any circumstances. There is always a chance of coming back. In 1981, the England Cricket Team were given odds of 500-1 against beating Australia after they had made a very bad start. The match was seemingly a foregone conclusion. England had all but lost. But then, Ian Botham came in to bat and turned the game on its head. Gradually, the odds changed and a remote

> When we were playing in the final nobody seemed to panic, even when New Zealand were taking quick singles and pushing the score along. I was just thinking what Steve was saying —
> just go with the flow and it will eventually come your way.
>
> *Jo Chamberlain*,
> *Member of 1993 World Cup winning England Women's Cricket Team*

chance of English victory became possible. With some fine bowling by Bob Willis in the final innings, England eventually scraped a famous victory. It was hard to believe. But they had done it. This was a marvellous display of mental toughness and the "never say die" attitude which world class performers often exhibit.

Most sports involve shifts in momentum whereby one side experiences a period of domination and then the other side enjoys a period on top. Staying focused and positive through these periods is an illustration of mental toughness. Concentration and confidence ensure this but can only be exhibited with effort and commitment.

So, ask yourself, do you fight to the bitter end? Can you maintain self-belief when you are performing badly? Is confidence under stress one of your strengths? If not, you need to work hard on your mental toughness training.

● 6 Positive body language

In sport, as in other areas of life, body language conveys messages about confidence, commitment, motivation and attitude. When an athlete drops the head or demonstrates bodily signs of anxiety, frustration or anger, strong messages are being given which can be extremely encouraging for opponents. It is far easier to be positive and confident when you know your opponent is feeling negative and dejected.

The importance of projecting a positive attitude with appropriate body language should not, therefore, be underestimated. Athletes should be aware of the signals they are sending their opponents and work hard to consistently display a confident and tough image. Keeping the head up, walking confidently, and projecting a positive facial expression is vital if you are to appear in control. It is common for athletes to report that they find it much easier to feel confident if they are exhibiting positive body language whereas if they drop their head and appear dejected, a negative attitude usually takes hold.

So, why not ask someone to observe your body language during training and competition? Watch yourself on video and compare your body language to that of a top performer in your sport. Do you look like you mean business? Do you look confident and ready to meet the demands of high pressure competition? And most importantly, do you maintain positive body language even when you're losing or playing poorly?

Overcoming fear of failure

When you have acquired the attribute of mental toughness, successful performance in pressure situations is possible. You will not be afraid of playing to win as opposed to playing not to lose. This is an important distinction in the world of competitive sport. Research has shown that some performers are motivated predominantly by a need for achievement and success. These individuals tend to seek out challenging situations which offer them this chance of feeling good about achieving a goal. They don't like losing, but they're not afraid to. They are usually the champions. Other athletes, however, are motivated predominantly by a fear of failure. They try very hard because they don't like to lose. But this fear of losing is so significant that they choose not to seek real challenges. Their performance is

> **If you're afraid of losing, then you daren't win.**
>
> *Bjorn Borg*, five times Wimbledon tennis champion

easily stifled. They would rather perform in an environment where their self-esteem is not threatened and success is pretty certain. These athletes tend to choke under pressure and do not display the qualities of mental toughness which we have so far been discussing. Athletes should closely examine their own sources of motivation and determine whether they would benefit from changing the focus of their competitiveness from a fear of failure basis to a desire for success basis. In other words, enjoy the competition for what it is and don't reserve your enjoyment for the occasions when everything goes your way. Be competitive and work hard to win, but don't worry too much if it doesn't work out. Be angry for a while if you wish but then bounce back and try hard again next time — perhaps with a different strategy.

Developing superior mental preparation

Having read the pages of this chapter, and considered your personal responses to the questions which have been posed, you may be asking how you can go about improving specific aspects of your mental toughness. The remaining chapters of this book are designed to help you do this. Work your way through the book methodically in order to acquire the basic skills of superior mental preparation. Then, perhaps with the assistance of your coach, you can begin to adapt some of the mental skills outlined to suit your own individual strengths and weaknesses. You must be prepared to spend time developing these skills. Be patient and the improvement will come but don't expect miracles overnight. Superior mental preparation is a skill — and as such, some people find it easier than others but there is room for improvement in everyone.

Mental skills training does not take the place of physical, technical or tactical training. It enhances these and increases the probability that what is accomplished through these forms of training will be evidenced in competitive performances. Learning mental skills will prevent the type of

Monica Wetterstrom, *multi-event international athlete*

When you have acquired the attribute of mental toughness, successful performance in pressure situations is possible

statement the cartoon character Charlie Brown made as he dropped a catch in baseball:

"My brain hasn't talked to my body in years".

Once you have a swing or a stroke that works reasonably well, your mental and emotional approach becomes about 95% of the package that determines how well and how consistently you score. That's a well-known, often-published, often discussed fact, but too many amateurs, as well as a few professionals, don't pay attention.

Ray Floyd,
former champion
golfer

Mental skills provide an athlete with the ability to allow the brain to talk to the body and vice versa. Mental skills provide an athlete with means for conversing, with the knowledge of when, and when not, to converse and the knowledge of what conversations work in different situations.

Athletes who have good mental skills are able to make anxiety work for them. They are able to stay focused at the critical moments. They do not get distracted by errors. They can often improve performance with less physical training time. They are confident in their ability even when things are going badly. And of course — they win more medals!

By utilising the skills outlined in this book, we cannot promise you a bag full of victory medals. The correct mental approach is no substitute for basic inherited physical ability. Positive thinking will not make you better than you have the physical potential to be.

> **One of the key techniques Bruce (Longden) has taught me is that at the highest levels of sport the difference between the performance of individual athletes is measurable only in tenths or hundredths of a second. Any technique that will tighten those fractions has to be used.**
>
> *Sally Gunnell*,
> *Olympic Gold*
> *Medalist and*
> *World Champion*
> *hurdler*

But, mental skills training CAN, AND DOES, maximise your chances of getting as close as possible to that potential. It can give you that final edge, those few percent, which so often mean the difference between winning and losing. In short, if you want to prepare as well as you possibly can, then mental training simply must be a part of that preparation.

A concluding thought to this opening chapter. It has been said that....

"Under pressure you can perform up to 30% better or 30% worse."

We hope that the skills and techniques presented throughout this book will assist you in moving towards the 30% better direction. The rest is up to you!

Chapter 2
Defining your goals: The motivation plan

The purpose of goals is to focus the attention. Vision expands the horizons; the greater the vision, the greater the goal that will be achieved.

Will Carling,
the most successful captain in English rugby history

Kicking off

The main goal of this book is to provide you with a mental game plan (MGP). By using this MGP, you will hopefully perform with greater consistency, and at a higher level. However, before you can begin your MGP you need to identify the main focus of the plan. The aim of this chapter is to help you identify the framework for your MGP with two simple techniques. Not only will these approaches be helpful now in designing your first MGP, but they will be just as useful when you come to redesigning your plan from time to time.

Les Ferdinand, *England and Newcastle striker*

Setting goals will always give you direction and purpose in training and competition.

Flicking through the chapters of this book, you will see that there are many different factors which contribute to the mental side of sport performance. With so many things to think of you are probably wondering, *where do I start?* When we consult athletes for the first time we are always faced with the same problem. To an extent, this problem is overcome simply through talking with athletes. However, you will not always have the luxury of access to a sport psychologist. So, there are other techniques that are used to help identify where athletes needs to focus their training, and two of these are outlined below to help you get underway in your quest to improve your mental approach to competition.

Of the two approaches we will outline, you may wish to use these in conjunction with each other, or you may prefer just one of the two approaches. Whichever way you decide to progress you should find that you will have identified the ideal programme content for you, at this point in time. We would recommend that you use both approaches, as this will give you the opportunity to really think about your mental game in detail, and use as much information as possible in finalising your first programme. Remember, assessing your MGP needs shouldn't be a one-off process. You should appraise yourself on a regular basis to be sure that you are constantly working to improve your mental game. Your needs will change throughout the course of a season, just as your physical and technical requirements change. Therefore, keep the results of the procedures to use for comparative purposes at your next point of self-assessment.

Identifying your MGP focus

Performance Profiling

In recent times sport psychologists have begun to concentrate on designing techniques to help athletes work out the most appropriate focus for their mental training. Probably one of the most frequently used of these techniques is Performance Profiling. This process is the idea of British sport psychologist, Dr Richard Butler, and in simple terms it allows you to

identify where your performance-related strengths and weaknesses are, so you can then develop a programme of training
which you feel will help your performance improve. Although
we are suggesting that you use this approach to help with
your mental training, there is no reason why you shouldn't
use it for other aspects of your training. Many athletes on
various British teams have been using this approach for all
aspects of performance for some time now, and both coaches
and athletes have found it a very useful addition to their
approach to competition and training.

The process of Performance Profiling is not a complicated one, and it is the simplicity of the process which often
appeals to athletes. The process gives you the opportunity to
reflect on your abilities and determine how you are progressing towards your ultimate sporting goal.

How profiling works

Use the blank Performance Profiling sheet provided (see
opposite) and follow these steps:

● 1   Identification of key performance attributes

Spend a good amount of time identifying all those factors
which contribute to peak performance in your sport. To help
you carry out this appraisal you may want to use one of the
following approaches: a) Identify the best performer that you
can think of in your sport and list all the qualities possessed
by that person which, when added up, make them the ultimate performer, or b) Think of yourself at the peak of your
potential and list all the qualities that you would need to
achieve to become that accomplished.

List all these qualities on the Performance Profile sheet.
You can be as specific as you like, and there is no need to limit
yourself to mental qualities. As you will see, fitness or technical qualities can often form the basis for your MGP, so these
will be just as important as the very specific mental qualities
you might identify. Give thought to all aspects of performance (e.g., pre-performance preparation, different stages

PERFORMANCE PROFILE   **Date** _____

QUALITY	Ideal level	Current level	Discrepancy Ideal-Current	Peak level

QUALITIES TO WORK ON:

1. _____

2. _____

3. _____

within performance) as these may help you build up a more detailed picture of just what contributes to your sport.

● 2   Rating of attributes

Having identified each of the qualities you need, start giving yourself targets to aim for in relation to each quality. In order to do this you need to give yourself an "ideal " rating for each of the qualities. The score you give each quality should be your target. Think how important each quality is in helping you become as good a performer as possible. Rate the quality on a 1 to 10 scale, with 1 being "not at all important" and 10 being "extremely important". Most athletes find that they usually rate everything as a 10.

● 3   Assessment of current status

Having considered your target, you now need to work out where you currently are in relation to your targets. Do this by considering your "current " rating for each of the qualities. Rate how far along the way you are to being at your target level. Be as honest as possible with yourself. Without a realistic rating, the programme that you design as a result of this process will not fully benefit you.

● 4   Establishing targets

Now subtract your "current " rating from your "ideal " rating score to work out the "discrepancy" score. This new score will determine which are your performance strengths and weaknesses. The higher the "discrepancy" score, the weaker you perceive your ability for the quality. We usually find that there are one or two qualities which really stand out with high "discrepancy" scores.

● 5   Prioritising targets

The next part of the process should be fairly straightforward. Having identified the major areas of performance weakness, you should now be able start planning how to go about strengthening these weaknesses. You will need to consider the "discrepancy" scores in some detail, and pick out the two or three scores which you feel need improving the most urgently. Any more than three and you will probably find you are trying to change too much, too soon. We often find that there are key qualities with which to work, and by improving these specific qualities there can often be a positive effect upon other areas of performance.

If your weaker qualities are easily identifiable as mental components of performance, then the relevant chapter(s) in this book should provide you with the tools to fine-tune your performance machinery. If the weaknesses relate to other areas of performance (e.g., physical, or technical) you should also look to build these up as this will often have a strong impact on your confidence and general attitude towards competition.

● 6   *Peak performance analysis*

An additional part of this process which athletes sometimes find useful is to identify a Peak Performance rating. In order to do this, think back to your best ever performance and rate the level of each quality on that day.

By comparing your Peak Performance rating to your Current rating you can usually draw one of two conclusions. First, if the Peak Performance rating is consistently greater than your Current rating, then you can use this as a basis for building confidence — you've been that good once, and with the right approach, you can be that good again. If your current rating is consistently higher than your Peak Performance rating then this should instantly fill you with confidence as you have already progressed from your previous highest levels.

An illustration of a Performance Profiling chart for a basketball player is provided on the following page. Use this to help you in constructing your own chart.

It is very likely that the factors which you feel are important to performance, and your relative performance strengths and weaknesses, will often change, so it is a good idea to use Performance Profiling regularly to help account for these natural changes and keep your training focused on your most critical needs. When you carry out a repeat profile, first

Performance Profile (Basketball example)

Date   <u>25 Jan, 1996</u>

QUALITY	Ideal level	Current level	Discrepancy ideal-Current	Peak level
Speed	10	7	3	8
Strength	10	6	4	7
Vertical jump	9	6	3	6
Range of shot	9	7	2	7
Funda-mentals	10	8	2	8
Staying calm under pressure	10	4	6	5
Confidence in shot	10	7	3	8
Stamina	10	8	2	9
Keeping focused	10	5	5	7
Reliable free throw	10	7	3	9
Agility	9	6	3	7
Good first shot	9	6	3	7
Aggressive	9	6	3	6

QUALITIES TO WORK ON:

1. <u>Staying calm under pressure</u>
2. <u>Keeping focused</u>
3. <u>Strength</u>

check to see if you still agree with all the qualities you listed, and also check to see if there are any new qualities which should now be included. Having done that, without looking at the scores you previously gave yourself, go through the rating process again to give you scores for comparison with your previous profile(s).

The Mental Skills Questionnaire

Another method which we regularly use to identify mental strengths and weaknesses in athletes, and to monitor progress, is via a Mental Skills Questionnaire. The Questionnaire is based on a much fuller version designed by two British sport psychology researchers from the University of North Wales. The Questionnaire measures seven important aspects of the mental side of sport performance. These are:

1. Imagery Ability.

2. Mental Preparation.

3. Self-confidence.

4. Anxiety and Worry Management.

5. Concentration Ability.

6. Relaxation Ability.

7. Motivation.

The Mental Skills Questionnaire consists of a number of statements about experiences associated with competitive sport. Read each statement very carefully and then circle the appropriate number to indicate the extent to which you agree with the statement. There are no right or wrong answers, and no trick questions. Be honest about your performance when you are answering each question in relation to your own sporting experience.

So, complete the Questionnaire on the following page now.

MENTAL SKILLS QUESTIONNAIRE

		Strongly DISAGREE ——				Strongly AGREE

Imagery Ability
1. I can rehearse my sport in my mind. — 1 2 3 4 5 6
2. I rehearse my skills in my head before I use them. — 1 2 3 4 5 6
3. It is difficult for me to form mental pictures. — 6 5 4 3 2 1
4. I can easily imagine how movements feel. — 1 2 3 4 5 6

Mental Preparation
5. I always set myself goals in training. — 1 2 3 4 5 6
6. I always have very specific goals. — 1 2 3 4 5 6
7. I always analyse my performance after I complete a competition. — 1 2 3 4 5 6
8. I usually set goals that I achieve. — 1 2 3 4 5 6

Self-Confidence
9. I suffer from lack of confidence about my performance. — 6 5 4 3 2 1
10. I approach all competitions with confident thoughts. — 1 2 3 4 5 6
11. My confidence drains away as competitions draw nearer. — 6 5 4 3 2 1
12. Throughout competitions I keep a positive attitude. — 1 2 3 4 5 6

Anxiety and Worry Management
13. I often experience fears about losing. — 6 5 4 3 2 1
14. I worry that I will disgrace myself in competitions. — 6 5 4 3 2 1
15. I let mistakes worry me when I perform. — 6 5 4 3 2 1
16. I worry too much about competing. — 6 5 4 3 2 1

Concentration Ability
17. My thoughts are often elsewhere during competition. — 6 5 4 3 2 1
18. My concentration lets me down during competition. — 6 5 4 3 2 1
19. Unexpected noises put me off my performance. — 6 5 4 3 2 1
20. Being easily distracted is a problem for me. — 6 5 4 3 2 1

Relaxation Ability
21. I am able to relax myself before a competition. — 1 2 3 4 5 6
22. I become too tense before competition. — 6 5 4 3 2 1
23. Being able to calm myself down is one of my strong points. — 1 2 3 4 5 6
24. I know how to relax in difficult circumstances. — 1 2 3 4 5 6

Motivation
25. At competitions I am usually psyched enough to compete well. — 1 2 3 4 5 6
26. I really enjoy a tough competition. — 1 2 3 4 5 6
27. I am good at motivating myself. — 1 2 3 4 5 6
28. I usually feel that I try my hardest. — 1 2 3 4 5 6

Scoring instructions

Work out your score in each of the sections by adding up the 4 numbers you have circled. Now calculate your percentage score for each category. Do this by dividing your score by 24, and multiplying the result by 100. For example, if you have scored 14 out of a possible 24 you would calculate your percentage score as follows:

$$14/24 = 0.58 \qquad\qquad 0.58 \times 100 = 58\%$$

The percentage scores you end up with do not represent a right or wrong score as you would get in an exam. These percentages simply show you where you are now, and you should use them in the future to assess if you have progressed from this starting point.

What to do now?

You should now have your seven percentage scores:

MENTAL SKILLS QUESTIONNAIRE RESULTS		
Date:	SCORE	PERCENTAGE
IMAGERY		%
MENTAL PREPARATION		%
SELF-CONFIDENCE		%
ANXIETY AND WORRY		%
CONCENTRATION		%
RELAXATION		%
MOTIVATION		%
MENTAL SKILLS TO FOCUS ON:		
1.		
2.		

As with the Performance Profiling, we usually find that there are one or two areas which usually stand out as relatively weak when compared with the general picture. Look through your results to see if there is an obvious point of weakness in your mental approach to competition. If there is an obvious weakness then you should turn to the relevant chapter(s) and decide upon the exercises that you will use to improve these area(s). Use the table below for a quick reference guide of where to look for each area.

AREA	WHERE TO LOOK
Imagery Ability	Chapter 4
Mental Preparation	All chapters—especially 9
Self-Confidence	Chapter 3
Anxiety and Worry	Chapters 3 and 6
Concentration Ability	Chapter 5
Relaxation Ability	Chapter 6
Motivation	Chapters 1 and 8

If there is not an obvious direction for your MGP yet then go back to the individual questions in the Mental Skills Questionnaire. Look just at the areas you scored less well on. See if there is one question that really highlights the reason for your weakness. This may stand out because it has scored lower than the other items in the category, or you just may feel that the question really sums up where your weakness usually shows itself. If there are specific question(s) which seem to be at the route of your weakness, then these should definitely form the foundations of your MGP. For example, if you gave yourself a low score on the question *"Being able to calm myself down is one of my strong points"*, this should instantly say to you that you need to do two main things. First, you need to learn techniques which allow you to control your arousal levels. Second, you need to develop these skills so that you can use them in a competition situation. With these two targets in mind you should easily be able to construct a plan of attack.

If your weaker scores represent lower ability across a whole area then you should look to build up your ability with a more general programme, which you will be able to do by detailed reading of the relevant chapter(s).

Setting your MGP targets

As with all forms of training, there is little chance that you will maintain quality mental training without a thorough consideration of where you want to get and how you will go about getting there.

Coaches, athletes, and sport psychologists will often be heard talking about goals. Coaches will often state the targets that they expect their team to achieve for a season. In a pre-performance interview, athletes might inform us of where they are aiming to finish in the approaching competition. Both these examples are a type of goal. Without appropriate goals we would not have any focus for training or competition, and if used well, a programme of goal setting can actually help to improve performance in training and competition.

We will outline the process of goal setting in relation to setting targets for your MGP. However, the basic rules can be easily applied to the other areas of your preparation, as well as competition itself. There are some important points to make regarding goal setting for competition, and these will be explained at the end of this chapter.

You will have identified performance qualities that you feel need most urgent attention. Having done this, you now need to design a structure which will allow you to strengthen those performance areas, as well as gain important feedback in relation to how well you are progressing. In order to give your MGP this direction and purpose there are a few simple rules you can follow to set yourself achievement targets. These are described below.

In chapter 10 you will see how to implement and stick to your MGP. In order to maximise the likelihood of sticking to your programme we would recommend that you use a detailed goal setting approach. In order to do this you will need to use the results from the Performance Profiling and/or the Mental Skills Questionnaire.

We will outline the general rules of goal setting now, and then give you a specific example of how these will help you to carry out your MGP more effectively.

Be SMART when setting goals

SMART (Specific, Measurable, Adjustable, Realistic, Time-based) is a useful acronym to remember whenever you are evaluating goals that you have set for yourself, or that you have agreed with your coach.

In order to assess the benefits of the SMART approach we will take, as an example, the goal:

"I will improve my mental aspects of performance."

This is a poor goal to set because it fails to satisfy nearly every SMART requirement. After considering each of the SMART factors we will propose a much more appropriate goal.

● *S is for Specific*

Whenever you set a goal you should be very clear in your mind of exactly what that goal relates to. If we consider our example goal it is very obvious that there is no specific target. 'Mental aspects of performance' encompasses a wide variety of topics. If there are several aspects which could be improved, then separate goals need to be set. For example, one goal might relate to increasing concentration skill, and another goal might relate to improving self-confidence. Always make sure that you identify your target area as precisely as possible. This also means that the extent to which improvement is desired needs to be stated. Simply stating that improvement is desired doesn't give a target of how much improvement will be sufficient. This point leads on to the next part of the acronym.

● *M is for Measurable*

Any goal that you set should always be capable of being measured in some way. If it cannot be measured, how can you assess if you are making any progress? Again, think back to our example goal — where is the measurement for this goal? There is none. So, somehow we have to find ways to measure our mental abilities. Ideally you should always use objective measures to assess goals. This approach is possible if you use the percentage scores from the Mental Skills Questionnaire to measure mental ability. However, it is also possible that we can use subjective measurement scales, which is not a problem, as long as the scale is stated very specifically, and you make sure you use the same evaluation criteria each time. If you want to assess your MGP progress regularly you can also use the subjective scale provided in the Performance Profiling process. If you always score yourself on the same 1-10 scale, using the same approach, you will be able to assess how well you are progressing towards you goal(s).

● *A is for Adjustable*

Goal setting is always described as a dynamic process, and as such you need to be able to alter goals. If your progress is faster, or slower, than had been originally hoped for, you need to be able to change your goals in order to set the most appropriate target. Again think of the example goal. As there is no way of measuring progress, it would not be possible to make alterations if the need arose. The importance of having adjustable goals is highlighted best through an example relating to physical performance. If you set a goal of taking 1 second off your personal best for 800 metres by mid-July and you become injured in June, it is obvious that the goal would be inappropriate due to training time being missed through injury. Therefore, fitness and performance potential would both decrease. Don't be afraid to adjust your goals if the situation demands it. Equally, if you make real progress in a short space of time, you may wish to extend your goal(s).

● *R is for Realistic*

Consider the example goal — *"I will improve my mental aspects of performance"*. Although there are many other things wrong with the goal, it can still be identified as being a 'realistic' target to achieve. It is not unrealistic to think that mental abilities can be improved. A common error, however, with goal setting is to set targets that cannot be achieved. It is essential that you set challenging goals, but these should not be so challenging that you never get to fulfil the goals. If you never manage to complete a goal, you will lose confidence in yourself, or give up trying.

If you haven't set yourself challenging goals, it's too easy to turn back and go home when it's a miserable day and training doesn't appeal. Goal setting is the key to motivation.

Kirsten Barnes, Canadian rower, and double Olympic Gold Medalist

As a simple rule, you should set goals that are sufficiently beyond your present ability to make you work hard and persist at reaching the goal over the set period of time. Therefore, when you are setting your MGP goals, be sure that they are realistic. Don't give yourself goals such as "I will improve my Relaxation ability score by 20% by the end of next week". It is very unlikely that one single week of relaxation training would produce such an effect. In order to make the goal challenging, but realistic, you could keep the same amount of target improvement, but change the amount of time to seven weeks, for example. This leads onto the last aspect of the goal setting acronym.

● *T is for Time-based*

All goals should have a specific time-frame. That is to say that you should always identify a point in time when the goal has to be achieved. Without this target date or time, a goal will have less motivational impact upon an athlete. With the example goal, the goal does not state when improvement has to occur. Therefore, it is unlikely that you would view achievement of the goal with any urgency or feeling of priority. You may even fall into the trap of perpetually saying that you'll begin your training programme tomorrow or next week.

There is another aspect to viewing goals as time-based. In general, there are three time-periods for setting goals: short-term, intermediate-term, and, long-term. If you view goal setting as a staircase, each individual step is a short-term goal. The bottom step can be seen as today and the very top of the staircase will be some specific point in time in the distant future.

By successfully climbing each of the steps you will progress up the staircase, towards your final goal. Once you are half way up the stairs, you will have achieved some of your intermediate goals. By achieving intermediate goals you will progress towards achieving your long-term goals.

There may be many steps to take on the way, but with this break-down approach, most goals start to become achievable. For your MGP goals, each session of mental training that you carry out could be seen as an individual step. After several weeks of training you should achieve your intermediate goal. Continuing the process over two months, for example, should ensure that you successfully achieve your long-term goal.

Therefore, when you set your MGP goals make sure there is a definite point in time by which your overall goal must be achieved. Decide upon some intermediate goals to act as progress checks. Finally, set specific weekly, or daily, targets for each mental training session. We have found that giving athletes a specific focus for each mental training session really does help with promoting quality sessions and increasing commitment to the programme.

Creating a SMART goal

Having highlighted some essential goal setting factors, we can now review the earlier goal — *"I will improve my mental aspects of performance"* — and provide an example of a more appropriate approach to goal setting. Note that the sample schedule below employs SMART goals that are **specific, measurable, adjustable, realistic,** and **time-based.**

SMART GOAL SCHEDULE

Long-term Goals

Goal 1.   Date of this goal: July 1st.

By September 10th I will have improved my concentration skill score on the Mental Skills Questionnaire by 20%, to 75%.

Goal 2.   Date of this goal: July 1st.

By September 24th I will have improved my 'positive second serve' rating on the Performance Profile scale from 4 to 8 out of 10.

Intermediate Goals

Goal 1.   Date of this goal: July 1st.

By August 5th I will have completed 25 concentration sessions. I will have improved my rating on the Mental Skills Questionnaire concentration skill scale by 10%. I will be using concentration training sessions prior to three of my seven weekly skill improvement sessions.

Goal 2.   Date of this goal: July 1st.

By August 19th I will be using positive thoughts in every training session prior to each second serve. I will have listed 10 positive thoughts in my confidence diary about my best serving performances. I will have developed my 'serving positive imagery' programme and will be using this in 3 sessions per week following initial relaxation.

Short-term Goals (Example of one week's training)

Goal 1.   Goals for week 8th-14th July.

Session 1: *15 minutes of serving with coach making distractions.* (Monday, 17.45)

Session 2: *10 minutes imagery session — performing against a distracting opponent.* (Tuesday, 18.00)

> Session 3: *10 minutes imagery of most focused ever performance.* (Thursday, after training)
>
> Session 4: *15 minutes as Monday* (Friday, after training)
>
> Session 5: *15 minutes — 5 mins as session 2, 5 mins as session 3, 5 mins as session 2* (Saturday, 18.00)
>
> Goal 2. Goals for week 8th-14th July.
>
> Session 1: *5 minutes imagery of county final. All positive second serves.* (Monday, before training)
>
> Session 2: *5 minutes viewing video compilation of players with a positive second serve.* (Wednesday, during lunch break)
>
> Session 3: *5 minutes imaging second serving like video compilation.* (Wednesday, 18.00)
>
> Session 4: *Write down 5 positive statements in confidence diary.* (Sunday, midday)
>
> Review all goals on Sunday. Achieved/not achieved.

Other important goal setting factors

As well as being SMART when you set your goals, there are several other factors worthy of attention. These will relate more to when you are using goal setting for competitions.

● Write your goals down

You should always write your goals down, and leave them in a visible place. Making your goals public in this way means that you can't hide from them and you have let everyone know what you are trying to achieve. If the people around you know what you are aiming for they can often be a big help in driving you on towards achieving your goals.

● *Choose controllable goals*

When you are considering your achievements in competition you should normally make sure that your goals are self-controlled. By this we mean that completion of the goals should be in your power.

The best way to explain this is to give examples of Process and Outcome goals.

Outcome goals relate to your finishing position in a race, or if you win or lose a competition. These type of goals are not wholly controlled by you. For example, you can run a personal best in a race, but if you have set an outcome goal which states you have to win that race, you have failed to achieve your goal, despite a superb performance. If you always set outcome goals it is possible that your confidence will often be dented.

Process goals are goals which are largely in your control. Aiming to beat your personal best would be a process goal. It is often the case that if you set challenging process goals, outcome goals will follow. For example, by running a personal best it is perhaps likely that you will win the race anyway.

Although it is sensible to set predominantly process goals, we would recommend that you also use outcome goals from time to time. It is often this type of goal that keeps athletes striving to be the best. It is highly unlikely that Linford Christie has been so dedicated over the past decade through following just process goals. Without the enduring desire to be the best in the world, he would not have been able to maintain his incredibly high standards.

So what happens when you are consistently winning? Well, goals can still play a part in your game. For example, Stephen Hendry has dominated the world of professional snooker for some years now. How does he maintain his drive? Hendry has two main goals to which he is still working. First, he plans to win seven world titles (beating the previous best of six). Second, he has a target of staying world number one until the year 2000! Hendry stated these goals publicly during the post-UK Open victory interview on BBC television in 1995.

**Stephen Hendry, the most successful snooker player in the history of the game.
His motivation to succeed continues by his constant setting of challenging goals.**

● *Be involved in your own goal setting*

As your goals have to be self-controlled, it is sensible that you set them yourself. With coaches and other performers around you in teams you may often find that other people are setting goals for you. If this is the case, try to get involved in the process so that you agree with the goals that are finally set for you. If you don't agree with the targets, then you will be unlikely to be motivated towards achieving the goals.

● *Review your goals regularly*

Finally, as is suggested in the above goal setting example, you should get into the habit of reviewing your goals on a regular basis. Sit down at the end of each week and assess how well you have achieved your original targets. Carrying out this regular assessment will allow you to identify early if your goals are being too lenient or too hard.

Get into the habit of using goals in all the aspects of your performance preparation. If you have a specific target to achieve for everything you do in relation to your sport it is very likely that the quality of all your training will improve. Improved quality will often lead to decreased quantity, so from a time-management perspective it might be sensible to spend an extra few minutes planning your goals to save wasting considerably more time carrying out low quality training.

The goal setting fundaMENTALs

1. *Be honest with your self-assessments.*

2. *Use the approach or approaches which most appeal to you.*

3. *Appraise your goals regularly — ideally, every 6-8 weeks.*

4. *Set SMART goals to maximise motivation, commitment and quality.*

5. *Design long, intermediate, and short-term goal setting schedules.*

6. *Assess your goals each week.*

Chapter 3
Positive thinking:
The confidence plan

Negative thoughts lead to a negative performance; the connection is as straightforward as that. The solution is to focus on the race. This means firstly to keep the concentration as unbroken as possible, and secondly to try to change any negative thoughts into positive ones.

Sally Gunnell,
Olympic Gold Medalist and World Champion hurdler

In order to perform consistently at a high level, and to cope with the inevitable pressures arising from involvement in competitive sport, athletes must believe that they are capable of meeting the demands of the challenge before them. They must believe that they have trained sufficiently to perform at that level. And they must maintain this high level of self-belief throughout the competition period. In our work as consultants, we have found that lack of self-confidence is the most common area in need of improvement in athletes of all ability levels. Even Olympic athletes experience self-doubt sometimes. So if this is a problem for you — don't worry, you're in good company.

"Steve Bull's programme of individual and team psychological skills allowed every member of the England Team to positively react to everything that came their way, and always remain firmly focused on the goal which was in all our minds — becoming World Champions!"

Karen Smithies, OBE
Captain of the England Women's Cricket Team, 1993
winners of the World Cup for the first time in 20 years

Sports self-talk

One of the most important determinants of developing and maintaining confidence is what athletes say to themselves. We call this *self-talk* and it is through this thinking that confidence is either enhanced or diminished. If athletes have a mental self-image of positive characteristics, positive perceptions, and positive traits, then they will be confident — and perform better. If negative characteristics, negative descriptions, doubt about ability or preparation creep in, then confidence is bound to drop — and of course, performance suffers.

Self-affirmation is a process of directing self-talk to affirm both the positive abilities and skills of the athlete, as well as the appropriate training and preparation which has gone before. Through the use of self-affirmation the athlete immerses in the conscious mind positive thoughts which are associated with producing excellent performance. Repeated use of such affirmations causes them to be planted in the subconscious mind and hence influence the athlete's personal perception of ability and skills. This enhanced perception increases confidence before, and during, competition and ultimately performance is likely to improve.

So, how can you go about improving your confidence? In our experience we've found a number of different techniques that seem to work well. Not all the techniques work for all athletes but we've found considerable success with each technique across a range of different sports.

Developing a personal list of positive affirmations

It is often the natural inclination of humans to engage in negative thinking and to doubt personal ability. Creating a personalised list of positive self-statements is the first step towards overcoming this habit. We encourage athletes to compile a list of, initially, between 4 and 8 affirmations relating to their sport performance. Examples of these types of affirmation are provided on page 44.

General sport-related affirmations

I am strong
I am confident in my ability
I have the skills needed to perform well
I can stay focused under pressure
My training is going well
I am progressing towards my long term goal
I can perform well in tough competitions
I feel good about my ability
I feel mentally strong
My coach is pleased with my progress
I like the challenge of competition
I can stay positive throughout competition

We get athletes to write their personal affirmations on a card and then read this card several times over on a daily basis. Eventually, the affirmations seem easier to repeat with conviction and the athlete becomes more comfortable with the whole process of positive thinking. They are then able to repeat the affirmations during training and competition as a means of sustaining positive thinking and confidence. In time, they find that their natural inclination is to think positively rather than doubt their ability. Some athletes like to record their affirmations on an audio-tape (or get their coach or another suitable individual to make the recording) and they play the tape before training or before going to sleep at night.

Develop your own affirmation list

● **1** Identify your own list of positive affirmations and write them on the chart provided (opposite). Make sure your list contains statements which have personal meaning and which refer to important aspects of skills, training and beliefs related to your sport.

● **2** Repeat the affirmations on a very regular basis — at least once a day.

PERSONAL SPORT AFFIRMATIONS

-
-
-
-
-
-
-
-
-
-

● 3 When you feel comfortable repeating the affirmations try using them in training and during competition.

● 4 Feel free to periodically change some of your affirmations if you wish. This may assist in keeping you focused on this important part of your mental training.

● 5 Keep doing your self-affirmation training even when you're feeling positive and things are going quite well. You never know what sort of challenge or pressure is waiting around the corner.

Develop personal sport achievement reminders

Another effective self-talk strategy involves keeping an up-to-date list of affirmations relating to successful sporting achievements. This acts as a method of personal verification of performance, improvement and worthiness. A sample list of this type is shown below. Note that this list includes satisfying personal performances which may not have resulted in medals or wins but which are excellent reminders of confident attitude. The more tangible outcome achievements are also included, however, because for some athletes these hold very significant meaning.

Personal sport achievement affirmations

I played a great game in the county trials last year

I was the youngest athlete selected for the regional squad

I performed brilliantly in those awful weather conditions at the Nationals

I came back strong after that terrible start in the first match of last season

I was voted Most Valuable Player twice last year

My fitness test results showed that I'm much stronger than before

I beat the favourite on her home territory in the London invitation match

I won a medal in January after just returning from injury

PERSONAL SPORT ACHIEVEMENT REMINDERS

-
-
-
-
-
-
-
-

Note: This list should be periodically updated

When compiling this, and indeed any positive affirmation list, it's important not to be modest. This list is for the athlete's use and need not be shown to anyone else. To generate a really strong sense of self-belief, an athlete cannot worry about feeling arrogant or big-headed. You have to believe in yourself and this must involve a certain amount of personal trumpet blowing. So, be bold and think strong is the advice we give to athletes if they are serious about improving their self-confidence.

When this personal achievement affirmation list has been compiled it can be used in a similar manner to the previous list and so the five steps can be applied again. However, we often find that the achievement list is most utilised when an athlete has experienced some sort of setback or when confidence seems to be waning. So, some athletes prefer to keep it in reserve for special occasions when it will have most impact.

It's important also to continually update this list. If further accomplishments are achieved they should be added as either additional, or replacements items. Some athletes also find it useful to extend these lists to other aspects of their life. In order to feel confident in sport, it's usually necessary to feel confident in yourself generally. Identifying achievements at school, university or work can be useful. Indeed, acknowledging successes relating to social and family life can be an effective way of boosting overall self-esteem which can then translate into confidence during sport competition. So it's worth considering your life as a whole and drawing as many positives as possible from different areas. They will all contribute to the creation of that ideal performance state where confidence is high.

Kate Pace, the 1993 World Downhill Ski Champion, provides an excellent adaptation of this. She described how she compiled a list which became her "treasure box". It was a list of all the good things in her life outside sport. In all, it was eight pages in length. She used to read it regularly referring to it as her treasure box. She explained how she carried the image of this box with her for one and a half years and how it made her feel good in the start gate. The start area in ski races can be a very stressful environment where negative thinking can easily creep in to a racer's mind. Kate would think about the contents of her treasure box as a means of making her feel relaxed and positive. If this technique appeals to you, why not create your own "treasure box" listing all the good things in your life. Then use the image of it to create a relaxed and positive attitude prior to competition.

Changing self-talk

We encourage athletes to analyse the content of their sport-related thinking and be on the look out for negatively framed statements. These statements must be reframed and replaced with positive ones. This, of course, makes sense but it is easier said than done. Changing self-statements is a skill and needs to be carefully considered and practised. The key to a successful reframing is twofold. First, don't try and deny or ignore that there is some degree of concern in the mind — this is too powerful to overcome in the short term. Rather, acknowledge that there is a real challenge in the situation but attempt to think about the challenge from a different angle. Second, always try to have a replacement thought ready which has been practised and rehearsed previously. This will not be possible for all situations but the more mental training which has been done, the more likelihood there is that the athlete will be equipped for an unexpected arrival of self-doubt and negative thinking.

The chart "**Changing self-statements**" on p. 50 shows examples of how negative self-statements can be replaced with positive ones without ignoring the challenge inherent in the situation. The chart "**Tips for changing self-talk**" on p. 50 shows examples of how important the opening words of these self-statements are, and provides examples of standard negative and positive sentence beginnings.

Using these sets of examples as a guide, make a list of the typical negative thoughts which you have during training or competition. Then try to reframe them into examples of positive self-talk.

Changing self-statements

Change from Negative self-talk	Change to Positive self-talk
"I'm worried about facing that opening bowler again."	*"I'll be OK against that opening bowler as long as I play off the front foot."*
"I just can't perform in wet weather."	*"I can perform in wet weather if I'm prepared to work at it."*
"I can't seem to hit a decent length today."	*"Relax and focus on the target area — the length will come."*
"I just can't get that mistake out of mind."	*"Give me another chance — I'll make up for it next time."*
"That referee has probably cost us the game."	*"Right, we'll just have to win this without any help from the referee — but we can still do it."*

Tips for changing self-talk

Negative opening	Positive opening
"It is difficult for me....."	*"It is a challenge for me....."*
"I can't....."	*"I can......if/provided I......"*
"If only....." *"I hope that....."* *"I trust that....."*	*"When....."*
"If I....."	*"When I....."*
"I'm worried about....."	*"I'll be OK.....if....."*

It's then very important that you practise thinking the positive self-talk so that when the negative thoughts enter your mind you can immediately replace them. You may find a skill called Thought Stopping helpful in this process.

THOUGHT STOPPING involves using a mental cue to block out uninvited negative thoughts. We have found that some athletes find it useful to create an image of a big red traffic light in their mind as a reminder to stop the negative thought. Others prefer to see a big sign with the letters STOP printed on it. Some others merely repeat (silently or aloud) the word STOP. The technique usually works even better if the athlete employs a physical mannerism at the same time as the STOP thought — such as slapping the thigh or clenching the fist. This acts as a physical cue to remind the athlete of the correct focus. Perhaps you can experiment to devise your own thought stopping mental cue. When you've chosen a suitable image and physical cue, you must practise using them many times before you find that it works in competition. And of course, you need to make sure you always follow your STOP image with the desired positive self-statement otherwise the negative one will re-emerge.

Competition-specific self-affirmation

Sometimes it's helpful to devise a specific affirmation plan for certain competitions. We have found that some athletes benefit from identifying statements which relate to a specific performance strategy they intend implementing or statements that act as attitude reminders. Examples of competition-specific affirmations are shown below.

Sample competition affirmations

I will maintain a fighting spirit throughout this match

My preparation has been excellent

Push forward as much as possible in the first quarter

Dig deep in the closing period

Persist down the left side

I am confident that an open game will work in my favour

I know I can handle the pressure of this tournament

If she gets ahead early, just stay calm and focused

Any anxiety I have will transform into energy and inspiration

If you think this technique may be useful for you, why not write several affirmations on the chart provided below prior to a competition? Read the card repeatedly in the days leading up to the competition to help you focus on specific aspects of your positive attitude. You may even wish to take the card to the competition with you and read it in the locker room as a final element of your mental preparation.

COMPETITION AFFIRMATIONS
Competition:
Venue:
Date/Time:
●
●
●
●
●
●
Note: Practise   these   affirmations   regularly   in   training

It's easy to forget the things you've been concentrating on in practice when you're immersed in the pressure of competition. The card — or cue card as some sport psychologists call them — will act as an important reminder of the types of thoughts you should be having as you prepare to compete.

The great New Zealand cricketer, Richard Hadlee, used to carry a cue card in his kit bag so that every time he opened the bag he was reminded of the right attitude towards competition. Hadlee's cue card (below) contains many statements worthy of close attention.

Richard Hadlee's Motivation

- *Fear is negative. Desire is positive.*
- *Your mind is your brain — it is better than a computer.*
- *Attitude is a frame of mind.*
- *Simulation — put yourself in a situation when you last did it.*
- *Visualise — dream and know you can do it.*
- *Believe — confidence breeds success.*
- *Think of the rewards of success — winning.*
- *Self-esteem — know your own worth/ability/value.*
- *Goals, aims, targets —be better than opposition — beat opponent.*
- *You must want to do it — power of positive thinking.*
- *Control — convert mental into physical/ actions.*
- *I'll do the testing. I won't be tested.*
- *Enjoyment.*
- *Robot — record and play the good things.*
- *Never get tired — just pleasantly weary.*
- *Winning is being happy with your performance, even if someone does it better.*

Richard Hadlee, in *At the Double* (1985)

When working with national junior tennis players we have
found that some players like to carry a cue card in their bag
which is left by the chair on which they sit during changeovers. Then, during some of the changeovers, they lean over,
pick up the card and read it through once or twice to remind
them of their match specific points of focus. On the card they
may have points relating to strategy or general positive attitude. Some players have reported to us that using the cards
was an effective method of teaching them how to stay positive
for long periods during competition. When they then became
better at staying positive, the cards became less necessary.

Focusing on the basics

**Don't let
perfection get
in the way of
performance
excellence ....
Just get on first
base.**

Doug Frobel,
former Major
League Baseball
player

There is an important lesson to
be learned from the quote by
Doug Frobel. Too many sports
performers enter the competition arena desiring perfection.
They are seeking an error-free
performance and rarely seem satisfied with their game even if
they win! They emerge from the
locker room mumbling about
some aspect of their performance
which needs tightening up. They
appear oblivious to the many aspects of their performance which
were commendable. They can
only dwell on those aspects which need further improvement.
Why? Because they set their sights too high. As Frobel says,
there are many occasions in sport when the most appropriate
attitude is one where the goal is to "do what is necessary" to
achieve the desired result. Yes, you will make mistakes. Sport
is about ups and downs. But it is still possible to achieve performance goals and feel very satisfied without being any-
where near "perfection".

In short then, an excellent focusing strategy to sustain
positive attitude is to concentrate on doing the basics well. So,

consider what the basics are in your sport. It may help to identify the "critical moments" in your competitive performance.
For Froebel, it was standing on the batting plate ready to re-
ceive the pitch. When you've identified the critical moments
you can think about the "critical cues". In other words, what
should you be focusing on during these critical moments.
Again, for Froebel it was getting on first base. He was not
dreaming of hitting a home run or thrilling the spectators with
an extraordinary performance — he was focusing on the
achievable goal of getting on first base. The home run may, of
course, happen. But if it does, it's a really pleasant bonus!

Now, there will be times when an athlete needs to set
sights higher. For example, if a boundary is needed off the last
ball of the match in cricket, or a 3 point shot in the final seconds of a basketball match. Under these circumstances, the
goals must be adapted accordingly, but these situations are the
exception rather than rule.

The performance review

The performance review list is a simple, yet very effective,
way of developing a positive attitude towards preparation
and performance. An example list for a tennis player is shown
below.

Sample performance review list for a tennis player

Good points list	Bad points list
High proportion of first serves in	*Dropped head for several games in first set*
Stayed focused on deuce points	*Second serve was quite weak into advantage court*
Stuck at game plan well	*Attacking lobs not deep enough*
Backhand slice was great	
High volleys are really improving	

We have found that it is particularly useful for athletes competing in individual sports but can also be used in team games. Basically, it involves finding about 15 minutes sometime in the 24 hours following a competition. The technique can be carried out alone, or in collaboration with a coach or team-mate. The athlete reflects on the performance which has just occurred and firstly compiles a list of all the things that went well. Each positive element of performance is recorded in a "good points" list. The list will vary in length and content but should include all aspects of the performance with which the athlete was satisfied. Then, the same process occurs for the negative elements of performance — a "bad points" list is compiled. When both lists (see opposite) are complete the following steps are completed:

●1   Read the "bad points" list carefully and consider how the elements on it can be improved in the future. Make some notes to assist discussion with a coach or identify how training may be modified to strengthen any weaknesses. In other words — get something positive from this list. Learn, and grow stronger, from mistakes, failure or sub-par performance.

●2   Throw the "bad points" list away and forget it. Some positives have emerged from it but otherwise it's history. These negative aspects of performance should now be consigned to the garbage disposal. Continually reflecting on them and brooding for days will decrease the chances of entering the next competition in a totally positive frame of mind and can even result in the same negative aspects of performance occurring again — simply because they've been thought about so much!

●3   Read the "good points" list carefully and recall the positive feelings associated with these successful elements of performance. Remember how it felt to perform like this and create a mental image of the different items on the list. Keep this list and either insert it in your training diary or pin it on your bedroom wall.

PERFORMANCE REVIEW LIST

Competition:

Venue:

Date/Time:

GOOD POINTS LIST:

-
-
-
-
-
-

BAD POINTS LIST:

-
-
-

Note: *Cut off bad points list and throw away after use*

● 4   Re-read the list again several days later or, indeed,
         whenever you feel in need of a confidence boost.
         Work hard to focus on the positives and recall the feel-
         ings associated with executing these positive aspects
         of performance. Even if it's only one thing. Remember
         it and use it to your advantage.

● 5   Next time you compete, focus on repeating the posi-
         tives. Accept that it won't all go your way but try to
         perform to your strengths.

Confidence modelling

Many world class athletes have explained how they have used
other performers as role models. They have pretended to be
the World Champion at whatever they are doing — training,
competing, preparing equipment, etc.. They imagine how the
World Champion would react in stressful situations and attempt to emulate that behaviour when they are in those situations. This modelling, of course, includes imitation of the
thought patterns and so can be an effective way of creating a
positive and confident attitude.

Watching videos of athletes who are a little better is another popular modelling strategy. This can foster a determined attitude whereby athletes are spurred on to train
harder and be more positive because they have an observable
goal to chase — i.e., the next level of achievement.

So, consider whether you can model yourself on other,
as yet more accomplished, performers in your sport. If you
feel comfortable with this strategy, try to emulate their behaviours and react in the positive manner in which they
would. Above all, present yourself as a motivated and optimistic athlete who is extremely professional in the approach to
performance.

Another effective use of video modelling involves compiling a selection of footage which captures your recent excellent performances. Watching this "highlights" video can then
be an enjoyable way of developing a very positive attitude towards future performances. The England rugby union team
have used this technique very successfully in the past — most

notably in dealing with the specific pressure of playing at Cardiff Arms Park, the Welsh national stadium, where the English record was very poor for many seasons.

If you do not have access to your performances on video tape, your own visualisation can be a worthwhile, and sometimes preferable substitute. Recalling your "finest hour" performances and reliving them through visualisation is a widely used technique for enhancing confidence. This technique is particularly effective for athletes who are very good at the skill of visualisation. You'll learn all about this skill in the following chapter .

Equipment doesn't think — so take control

This technique is very straightforward. It involves athletes reminding themselves that sports equipment does not think. A tennis racquet does not know it is at match point. A golf ball does not know the green is surrounded by bunkers. A pair of skis is not aware that it is in the Olympic Games. Athletes must feel that they are in control of their equipment rather than the other way around. They must not feel at the mercy of their environment. The

The first thing to do is try and enjoy it. To like it, like the place I'm in, try to feel very confident in myself.
Nicola Fairbrother, *World Lightweight Judo Champion*

I love competition. It motivates me, stimulates me, excites me... I just love to hit that baseball in a big game.
Reggie Jackson, *Former baseball star*

Skiing is a battle against yourself, always to the frontier of the impossible. But most of all, it must give you pleasure. It is not an obligation.
Jean-Claude Killy, *triple Olympic Gold Medalist*

golf ball will react according to how it is hit — not according to the number of bunkers around the green. So, try to focus on executing the skill rather than on how much pressure is involved in the execution. The ball is not nervous — it's just waiting to be hit! In short, you'd be confident if it was a practice day when the technical demands are basically the same. So be confident now, and take control. Make things happen — don't wait for things to happen!

Confidence reminders

It is important to emphasise that, like most aspects of mental training, positive thinking is a skill which must be practised on a regular basis. Even if you're going through a stage of feeling very confident it's still important to keep working on the positive approach. Keep practising some of the techniques suggested in this chapter so that when critical competitions arise, it will be far easier to sustain this positive attitude through periods of intense stress and pressure. Getting coaches and team-mates to remind you of the techniques which work best for you is also worth remembering. Time spent revising positive thinking skills is, in our experience, never wasted. Compiling a short reminder sheet for big competitions can be useful for many athletes.

An example of this is shown opposite — a sheet we gave to the England Women's Cricket Team prior to the World Cup in 1993. The sheet followed five years of mental training work and was devised to remind the players of different strategies they could employ if they experienced confidence problems.

There was no doubting the confidence of this team before, and during, the World Cup in 1993. They chose the Tina Turner song "Simply the best" as their theme tune and played it full blast before and after all their matches. They caused quite a reaction on the day of the final, when they ran onto the field at Lords — it is usual for teams to walk sedately onto the field. They were there to do business and gave every impression of a team who were going to take control of the match in a confident manner. They did just that and became World Champions.

Confidence Recovery Strategies — Women's Cricket World Cup

1. BEST-EVER PERFORMANCE MEMORIES
   ☆ recall a great innings
   ☆ recall a great bowling spell
   ☆ recall some great fielding
   ☆ recall general feelings associated with these

2.. EVALUATE YOUR SELF-TALK
   ☆ am I thinking negative thoughts?
   ☆ identify 2 positive things about your ability right now
   ☆ identify 2 positive things that you will do next time you are on the field

3. WHAT CAN I CONTROL?
   ☆ what have you been worrying about that is outside your control
   ☆ identify three things that you CAN control right now

4. WHAT WOULD THE IDEAL PLAYER DO?
   ☆ consider how the ideal cricket player would behave in this situation
   ☆ pretend to be the ideal player — play the role

5. RE-STATE YOUR POSITION
   ☆ remember that you're on the national team playing in the World Cup and that YOU GOT SELECTED
   ☆ review your ability and remind yourself of how good you really are

6. EQUIPMENT DOESN'T THINK
   ☆ remember that the bat and the ball are unaware of the World Cup — they will react the same

And . . . . ENJOY YOURSELF!

Enjoy the challenge

Although the final confidence tip we're suggesting, this
should not imply that enjoyment is the least important element in the positive thinking process. We think it is a crucial
part of an athlete's involvement in competitive sport, whether
it be at the professional, serious amateur or recreational level.
Much of the time, enjoyment and confidence go hand in hand.
It's extremely difficult to feel positive about your ability if you
are not enjoying yourself. This lack of enjoyment will manifest
itself in various forms — each of which will chip away at overall confidence.

We once heard of an international coach who would not
let athletes smile or laugh while training. This coach felt that
this would be evidence of poor concentration. We firmly disa-
gree with this approach and whilst we fully acknowledge the
importance of absolute concentration at the right times, we
feel that athletes must enjoy themselves along the way.

We particularly encourage the athletes with whom we
work, to enjoy "the great white of competition". We encourage
them to enter the competition arena looking as if they are ex-
cited about the prospect of competing. Then, during the actual
performance, we encourage athletes to use their body language to give a message of positive attitude and enjoyment of
the challenge. Even when things aren't going so well, we encourage them to focus on enjoying the challenge of digging
their way back.

So, start enjoying the challenge of tough competition.
Grit your teeth and hang in there all the way to the bitter end.
Enjoy the whole process and compete with a determined
smile on your face!

The positive thinking funda*MENTAL*s

● 1. *Develop your ability to use positive self-talk by devising a range of affirmations for different situations and challenges.*

● 2. *Use thought-stopping, or any other successful technique, for eliminating negative self-talk but always have replacement positive statements ready to use.*

● 3. *Focus on getting the basics right — don't expect absolute perfection every time you perform.*

● 4. *Review performance, learn from the negatives but then dismiss them and remember the positives.*

● 5. *Model yourself on other successful, confident performers who stay positive in pressure situations.*

● 6. *Remember that equipment doesn't think.*

● 7. *Enjoy the challenge of tough competition.*

Chapter 4
Visualisation:
The imagery plan

Visualisation. It has been called 'going to the movies' and it may be the most important part of your mental package.

Ray Floyd,
winner of the PGA, Master's and US Open
golf tournaments.

What is imagery?

The term imagery is commonly used in sport psychology. But what is it? It is not uncommon to see skiers or high-jumpers prior to performance with their eyes closed making slight movements. These athletes are using imagery to aid their performance. They are simply playing over in the mind the run to come, or the jump they are about to execute. Simply then, imagery relates to a process of seeing yourself performing or practising a sport related skill, or imagining yourself competing in a certain situation. Although imagery refers to "seeing" in the mind's eye, it is very important to point out that the most effective imagery goes beyond simply seeing a skill being performed. Well practised imagers will incorporate the sensations of hearing, smelling, tasting, and most important of all, feeling, into imagery sessions. The more detail that can be

65

"Before a big match I try to visualise myself in different situations in different parts of the field. I will spend a long time practising kicks from those areas of the field where we plan to attack."

Rob Andrew, MBE, the world's most capped fly half and England's leading points scorer in international rugby

included in the sessions, the more impact the training is likely to have. Remember this point for later in the chapter when you identify your imagery training contents.

In essence, imagery is the reproduction, in the mind, of all the relevant sensory information which contributes to the successful execution of a skill, or the correct behaviour for a specific situation. Through the regular use of this mental skill, athletes can augment their training and performance in many different ways. The table below shows some of the ways in which imagery can be used by athletes to assist with competition preparation.

Different uses of imagery in sport	
Imagery use	**Examples**
Mental practice of specific performance skills.	Imaging of a back-hand volley.
Improving confidence and positive thinking.	Imaging previous, successful performances.
Tactical rehearsal and problem solving.	Imaging basketball set-offences.
Controlling arousal and anxiety.	Imaging relaxing images to calm nerves.
Performance review and analysis.	Reviewing a match for strong and weak points.
Preparation for performance.	Imaging of performing well in different conditions — weather, opponents, luck, officials.
Within pre-performance routines.	Imaging a successful conversion attempt during pre-kick preparation.
Maintaining mental freshness during injury.	Imaging your golf swing when unable to physically practice.

> I am often seen before a race lying on my back in a bit of shade, my eyes closed. I'm not catching forty winks. I'm thinking about the race, preparing mentally for it. In the last few moments before the race begins you will usually see me looking straight ahead down the track. To some people it might seem like an aggressive stare, but in reality I'm simply visualising what I have to do.
>
> *Sally Gunnell,*
> *Olympic Gold Medalist and World Champion hurdler*

> My visualisation has been refined more and more as the years go on. That is what really got me the World record and Olympic medals.
>
> *Alex Bauman,*
> *Double Olympic Swimming Gold Medalist*

Why does imagery work?

Using imagery is very much like having your own "Virtual Reality" system in your head, which is connected directly to your body. When you image something in your mind's eye there is strong evidence to suggest that the muscles you would use to perform the skill are activated at a very low level. This muscle activation is not enough to make the movements you imagine, but a "blue-print" for the movements or situations is laid down. The more you image, the stronger the blue-print becomes, and the more likely you are to produce the correct response in the heat of competition. Therefore, by making regular use of this 'on-board system' you can effectively train both your mind and body to perform specific skills, more consistently, and across more situations. Equally, if you are using imagery to help improve confidence, or during preparation for performance, the more you see yourself performing to the best of your abilities, the greater the likelihood is that you will actually perform in that confident manner during performance.

What should you see?

When you image it is likely that you will see yourself performing in one of two ways. Some performers image from what is called the **internal perspective**. This simply means that when you imagine yourself performing, you create an image which replicates exactly what you see during a performance, i.e., you are looking from inside you, to the outside world. Internal imagery is thought to be most suitable for mental practice of specific skills, although as you will see, there are no rights and wrongs with imagery training.

If you don't naturally image from the internal perspective it is likely that when you image you use the **external perspective**. External imagers will create a picture in the mind in which they see themselves as if they were watching the performance on video, i.e., an external imager watches themselves performing from outside. This type of imagery can be very useful for imagery sessions which are focusing on tactical rehearsal or performance reviews. It is also useful for athletes competing in

Another thing ... that gets you to the point where you are one of the elite, is the ability to visualise not only the way it looks when you are going down, but how it feels... the muscle tension that you actually go through when you make the turns, and to experience what attitude your body is in .... I feel what things will feel like and see everything run through in my head. I have a moving picture with feelings and sensations. When I'm doing these mental runs... if I make a mistake, I'll stop the picture and back it up. Then I run it through and usually get it right second time. I run through the entire course like that. This ability is sort of an ingrained thing. It takes years and years of practice of visualisation.
Steve Podborski,
former World Cup
Downhill ski
champion

> I do a lot of imagery, seeing myself playing and performing well and making shots in my own mind both in training and before a game. I always do it before I play a game, during the afternoon rest, or when I lie in bed at night. I close my eyes and see myself going through motions and making every shot. Sometimes I like to look at it like I am watching it through a T.V. and I also like to watch it from my own eyes so that I can see everything happening from the inside.
>
> *Jay Triano*,
> *Captain of Canadian*
> *1984 Olympic*
> *Basketball Team*

judged sports where an external assessment of style is an important element of performance such as in figure skating or gymnastics.

Although sport psychologists think that the different perspectives are more useful in certain sessions than in others, there are no hard and fast rules. If you naturally begin to use one of the perspectives, this is likely to be your preferred approach, and you may find it difficult to switch into the alternative perspective. This is a very common occurrence, and both perspectives can produce positive results, whatever you are trying to achieve with your imagery training. In time, and with regular practice, you can improve your ability to image in different perspectives, although the overall effectiveness of your imagery training will not be limited if you only use one perspective.

How often should you use imagery training?

There are no firm rules to follow in order to answer this question. As all sports are so different, imagery sessions will all have different contents and objectives. One rule that you can follow in the early stages of your imagery training is to focus on short sessions on a regular basis. If you can find five minutes once or twice a day, this should help get you on the road to becoming a skilled imager. Once you feel you are ready to progress, then you can increase the length and complexity of your sessions.

Mental practice of specific performance skills

Perhaps the most common use of imagery is the rehearsal of a skill in the mind. The skill can be one which you are attempting to improve, or a well learned skill which you want to adapt for a particular situation. For example, a golfer may wish to develop a controlled fade. Through repeated imagery of the correct technique the skill could be worked on when away from the practice range. If this same player already had the skill to produce the controlled fade then imagery could be used to rehearse playing the shot on specific holes, or at high pressure points in a competition. Through repeatedly seeing yourself performing something in the correct manner, you are increasing the likelihood of performing the skill correctly when it comes to putting practice into action. Think of the number of times you have imagined something going wrong and then it usually does,

As for success imagery, I didn't do as much imagery of being on the podium as I have heard some athletes do. But I would imagine to myself, "How would a champion act? How would a champion feel? How would she perform on the line?"

Linda Thom,
1984 Olympic
Shooting Gold
Medalist

I have always done imagery... The feeling is what you are after, rather than just picturing it. It was through actually feeling it in my mind that I started to make all my jumps consistent.

Brian Orser,
1986 Figure
Skating World
Championships
Silver Medalist

> **Hugh and I would visualise our race. We would have a competition to see who could come closer to the real time. One of us would visualise and the other would hold the stop watch.**
>
> ***Alwyn Morris**, 1984 Pairs Kayak Olympic champion*

> **I never hit a shot even in practice without having a very sharp, in-focus picture of it in my head. It's like a colour movie. First I 'see' the ball where I want to finish. Then the scene quickly changes and I 'see' the ball going there. Then there's a sort of fade-out, and the next scene shows me making the kind of swing that will turn the previous images into reality.**
>
> ***Jack Nicklaus**, champion golfer*

in quite spectacular fashion. All you are doing with imagery is making this self-fulfilling prophecy work *for* you by imagining things going right for you. The more you see things happening the way you want them to, the more likely they will be to actually go right for you. Think to yourself, *"Are there any skills or situations in which I feel I would like to improve my performance?"*. If you can identify any, then this type of imagery training could be included in your mental training plan.

Improving confidence and positive thinking

As you have seen in chapter 3 with the Confidence Plan, using previous performances can be a very powerful way to help build your self-belief. If you have made lists of your previous best performances, or positive performance attributes, these could be the basis for a confidence building imagery programme. Replay the images of success in your mind on a regular basis. Take each item from your sport achievement reminders list and see yourself back in that situation again, performing to the best of your ability. We have found that athletes enjoy reviewing these positive items, as in the most part, a great deal of time is spent reviewing negative aspects of competitions. Constantly reminding yourself of all the good performance points by re-living them through imagery provides a positive platform from which to prepare before competitions.

As well as using the positive images prior to competition, you can use the images to help you with positive thinking during competition. If you are faced with a difficult situation, tricky shot, or tough opponent, for example, a positive image of a previous success in a similar situation can often help you to maintain a confident frame of mind. For example, a tennis player may be faced with a tough tie-break in the opening set of an important match. During the change-over preceding the tie-break the player may recall a previous match when a similar situation was dealt with successfully. The player would review the previous match, focusing on the confident feelings associated with playing well in the tie-break. Former world snooker champion Dennis Taylor recently won an important match 9-8 against Darren Morgan in the UK championship, having been 5-8 down. Taylor stated that during this game he recalled a previous tournament final in 1987, against Alex Higgins, in which he came from 5-8 down to win. Remembering that previous performance gave him the confidence to repeat the feat some eight years on.

Tactical rehearsal and problem solving

To a greater or lesser extent, all sports require different tactical approaches. In team sports the execution of tactical patterns are crucial to optimal performance. Each player on an American football team, or basketball team, has to know in great deal offensive or defensive patterns. If one player makes an incorrect move, the whole team will usually suffer. Imagery can be a very useful skill to help athletes memorise these

> I learned to play back successes in my mind, not as a spectator, but actually going through it all in the middle. I would recreate the day in question and everything about it - the weather; the state of the game; the other players around me; whatever was occupying my mind outside the game at that particular time, etc.. The principle is that if you've done it once, there's no reason why you shouldn't go out and repeat the performance.
>
> *Richard Hadlee*,
> *former international cricketer and world record holder for wickets in Test matches*

movement patterns. Learning of these movements can continue away from the training ground ready for when the team gets together. The more the athletes can familiarise themselves with their roles, the easier it will be for them to get the plays right during training and competition.

Even in individual sports tactical rehearsal can be very important. Using this approach it is possible to prepare yourself for almost any eventuality during competition. Having considered the situation before you will increase the probability of being able to cope effectively when you are actually faced with it. We find that on the whole athletes have particular tactical strengths, and if a performance doesn't allow these strengths to be used, then quite often anxiety will increase, confidence will drop, and performance will suffer. If you regularly image different scenarios you should increase your confidence to deal with less than favourable situations.

To an extent, this type of imagery training is teaching yourself how to alter your approach to competition if needed. As a development of this, we have found that it is often useful to have athletes imagine themselves in problem situations and practice how they would get themselves back in contention again. For example, a squash player might imagine being at match-point down and coming back to win; a basketball player might imagine playing against a particularly aggressive opponent; a soccer player might imagine being forced to play in an unfamiliar position. To give a highly developed example of how problem-solving imagery can be used, one Olympic wrestler with whom we worked, reported that he used this approach when he was actually competing. If he found himself in a hold, he would quickly visualise the position he was in as if he was a spectator. Using this external perspective he was able to work out how to get out of the hold, and having executed his mental rehearsal of the escape, he would then execute the problem-solving move.

As we have stated, competition is never a smooth process, and through using imagery in this way you can prepare yourself for coping with the lows so you can then make the most of the highs. Think about how prepared you are to deal with the unexpected, or think of previous occasions where you have been thrown by something not going to plan. See if there is a place for this type of imagery training in your mental game plan.

Controlling arousal and anxiety

You will see later in the book, in chapter 6, that anxiety and arousal often play an important part in deciding the outcome of a competition. When all things are equal, the player who deals best with the pressure is usually the one who triumphs. There are many ways to deal with anxiety and arousal but imagery has an important role in reducing performance worries. We have found that some athletes enjoy using images of relaxing places to help them achieve a relaxed state of mind. You might want to imagine, for example, relaxing on a beach, or being in a favourite tranquil place such as in a forest or up a mountain. Whatever the image you chose, make sure it is one that you associate with very relaxed feelings, and once you have carried out your mental warm-up, imagine that you are in your relaxed place and focus on all the positive feelings associated with being in that place. You should find that by getting your mind relaxed, your body should follow suit. You

Gabriella Sabatini, former US Open tennis champion

Skilled imagers can visualise so effectively they often feel like they are really competing

may want to use this type of imagery training from time to time to add some extra variety to your programme. You will still be enhancing your imagery skill, but you will give yourself a break from performance related imagery.

In the same way that imagery training can help to give you an air of confidence when going into performance, you can also use it to help get you into your optimal performance zone. When preparing for competition you can spend a few moments imaging yourself performing in a relaxed manner. As with the confidence building imagery, you may want to use a past performance to provide you with the relaxed images. An equally effective technique can be to select an athlete who has a well known relaxed approach to competition and imagine yourself performing in the same way. So, consider whether you might benefit from this type of imagery training. It might not be something you choose to use all the time, but if you are familiar with the skill, then it is something else to add to your mental training kit-bag which you can pull out and use when the need arises.

Performance review and analysis

Most of the imagery training that has been suggested so far relates to getting you ready for competition. However, imagery can be just as useful after you have finished a performance. During the few hours after competition it is often a good idea to go through a detailed imagery session of your performance to review it for strengths and weaknesses. Using imagery in this way should be helpful for making your performance review list introduced in chapter 3. It is often worth spending this short amount of time carrying out a structured review of your performance in detail, rather than pondering frequently on the performance for several days afterwards.

Within pre-performance routines

The importance of pre-performance routines is covered in chapter 5 of this book. Think to yourself, could you use imagery in preparing for specific skills in your sport, e.g., tennis serve, rugby place kick, soccer penalty/free-kick, netball shot, hockey short-corner? The list could go on and on, but the connecting factor is that imagery can be used in the few seconds prior to the execution of all these skills. Getting into the habit of seeing yourself execute a skill to the best of your ability immediately before actually doing it can really get your mind focused in on the job. The imagery will serve to get you to the appropriate arousal level, give you the necessary confidence, and re-affirm your performance cues. Look at chapter 5 to see how to establish your own pre-performance routine.

During periods of injury

Perhaps the must frustrating periods in an athlete's career are those times when injury occurs and there is no possibility of competing or training. It is at this time that imagery training can often be of most benefit. Paradoxically, we have found that this is usually the time when athletes stop doing their imagery training. The usual thought process is, 'well I'm not doing any physical training, so why should I bother with mental training?'. The best reason for carrying on with your imagery training is that it will help you stay mentally sharp, and mentally prepared for performance when the time comes to begin playing again. Cal Botterill, a Canadian sport psychology consultant, has often used team imagery training with injured ice-hockey players to keep them feeling part of the team and focused on their roles for when they can return to the line-up. He has even developed the term 'dream team' for these athletes in order to give them a positive identity.

In many cases, the events that have caused an injury might lead to a confidence crisis when faced with the same situation on returning to the heat of competition. It is unwise to return to competition before your body is ready to face the rigours of performance. Just as importantly, you shouldn't return before your mind is ready. Therefore, it is a good idea to combine your physical and mental rehabilitation during your recovery period. You will see in chapter 7 that there are often difficulties with sticking to the physical rehabilitation, so why not combine some confidence building imagery with your rehabilitation exercises to relieve the monotony. Look at chapter 7 to see how else imagery training can be used to assist with injury rehabilitation.

Making the most of imagery

Having decided on the focus of your imagery training, there are several pointers you need to follow in order to make the most of your "Virtual Reality" system. These are rules you should follow when you are first starting your programme. Once you are familiar with how imagery works best for you, some of the rules may no longer apply. A good tip at this stage is that you shouldn't be afraid to experiment with your imagery training once you have a grasp of the fundamentals of the skill.

● *Mentally warm-up*

As a general rule, if you want to have good quality imagery sessions, you will normally need to precede the session with a brief period of preparation. Just as you thoroughly prepare for physical training by warming-up to maximise the quality of a session, you should take the same approach to your imagery training. Whenever you are going to carry out an imagery session, make sure you are not going to be interrupted. Having found a place where you won't be disturbed, you can mentally warm-up simply by getting in a comfortable position (standing up, sitting or lying down), and by focusing on a slow, steady breathing rhythm for a few moments. During this time your body should begin to relax, and you can get a clear focus in your mind of what you are going to achieve in the session. Having done this you should be ready to begin a good session of imagery training.

● *Maintain a positive approach*

Imagery can have a profound influence upon performance, and if you make the most of it, it can be a powerful ally. As well as being a positive influence upon performance, the potential negative influence should be pointed out too. Think of a golfer who pictures an approach shot going into a lake. Having made this picture it is not surprising that nine times out of ten the ball will actually plop straight into the lake. If you sow a seed of doubt with a negative image in your mind, it is very likely to grow into the real thing in no time at all. Therefore, at all times, try to have a positive image of what you definitely know you are capable of achieving For example, see the ball landing straight on the green, rather than an image of something which you hope won't happen. Remember, seeing is believing, and this is very much the case for imagery. See something in your mind's eye that you want to achieve, and this will give you the positive frame of mind to actually achieve that target. See something that is negative and you will soon make yourself believe that the negative outcome is the only result you are likely to experience. Therefore, if ever you find yourself having excessive negative images, stop yourself, try to replace the image with a positive one, believe in the image, and then go for it.

● *Image in 'real-time'*

Having fully prepared, there are also important points relating to the content of the imagery you use during each session. Whatever you are imaging, you should always attempt to go through the skills you are practising at the speed you would actually execute them. Ski racers can image training and competition runs to within fractions of a second of the actual time taken when physically performing. Likewise with bobsleigh performers. Figure skaters and gymnasts can image their performance routines with amazing accuracy and track athletes image with a high degree of precision and detail. Running through skills too fast, or too slow, will probably not give you full benefit from your imagery training, as you will not be familiarising yourself with how things will actually happen when you are faced with them. This may seem like an easy task to fulfil. Just to highlight how difficult imaging in real-time speed can be, imagine yourself carrying out a task you are very familiar with, such as walking along a familiar path, or making a cup of coffee. Time how long it takes you to imagine the task, and then compare this time to how long it really takes you. You may be quite surprised by the results.

As has been outlined, imagery helps to lay down the muscle "blue-print" for skills. Imagery will also provide you with a mental map relating to the timing of skills. Timing is essential to the execution of most sporting skills, and therefore, the more familiar your mind and body are with the 'real-time' sequences involved within the skills, the better prepared you will be to perform the skill. Using imagery at the 'real-time' speed will help get your mind and body in 'sync'. With this increased familiarity with all the elements of the skill you will be more likely to produce the correct technique during performance.

● *Feel the movements*

It was mentioned earlier in this chapter that one of the most important aspects of imagery training is to focus on the 'feel' of the movements. If you can focus on this 'feel' element when imaging you will provide the body with more information to help make up the muscle 'blue-print' for the movements. You can do this by focusing on how all the appropriate muscles feel throughout a skill, but just as importantly you should concentrate upon other important factors such as the weight, texture, and shape of equipment you might be using. As a way of developing this aspect of imagery training, we often encourage athletes to carry out the training in their sporting environment, or whilst actually holding any relevant equipment. For example, shooters will image successful shots whilst actually holding their gun, or tennis players will image strokes they are trying to perfect whilst holding their racket. In the early stages of an imagery training programme this can often provide more valuable sensory information to enhance the quality and clarity of your images.

You have already seen how imagery should usually be carried out in a relaxed position and state of mind. However, it is sometimes useful to orient yourself as you would be when performing the skill you are rehearsing, as this will help you focus more on the 'feel' element of the task. Furthermore, we have found that athletes sometimes like to actually perform the skill, and then carry out an instant replay of the skill in their mind. Using this approach, the information relating to physical sensations is still very much in the mind, and can be recalled much more easily during the image. In turn, it is often the case that the information you attend to during the imagined skill will provide you with key points to focus on when you are actually carrying out the skill. Therefore, combining both physical practice and mental practice can often help with improving your ability to image, as well as helping to refine the skill you are trying to perfect.

● *Use all the senses*

As well as making sure you really feel the movements you are imaging, we recommend to athletes that they also try and incorporate as many of the other senses as possible into their imagery routines. Some senses will be more relevant than others. However, rather than just 'seeing' the picture, try to include typical sounds, smells, or even tastes into your routines. Also, try to image in colour. The more realistic you can make the content of the imagery session the more impact it is likely to have on your performances. The more you use imagery, the more you will find that these other senses become easier to use. To work on using all your senses, begin by imaging something that you are very familiar with. Perhaps you could use a particular venue, or situation. Try to build up as detailed a picture as possible. Go through the routine several times, focusing on a different sense each time. Eventually, you should find your skill increasing, and you will be able to build up a complete sensory picture.

● *Focus on quality training*

The key to successful imagery, as with other mental training techniques, is to make sure all your sessions are quality sessions. We find that in the early stages of learning imagery, athletes will often continue sessions when they are finding it hard to maintain concentration. As a result, the quality of their imagery decreases, and this will often result in feelings of frustration because it appears that they are not improving their imagery ability. As a result we often find that the best thing to help this is to use short duration, high-quality sessions, on a frequent basis. For example, rather than aiming for a ten minute session of performance related imagery, it is often better to try and carry out five two minute sessions throughout the course of a day. As you become skilled at imagery, you will find that you can hold concentration on the skill for longer, but in the early stages, this little and often approach helps to promote quality training. If you are carrying out a session of imagery training and you feel you are losing concentration, first, stop the image you are going through. Next, remain relaxed for a short while without any imaging. Finally, gear yourself up to focus on a final, high-quality run through of your image for that session. Using this approach, you should always finish a session with a positive feeling, having carried out good quality imagery throughout.

● *Use video*

In the early stages of imagery training, we find that the use of video can often help athletes to increase the quality of their imagery. The approach is very simple, and you don't necessarily have to have video of yourself performing. We suggest that athletes have video of top performers, or themselves, carrying out a skill, or performing in a specific way. The athlete plays the video sequence through once, and freezes the film. Next the athlete images the same situation, substituting themselves into the place of the performer on the video. The video-clip is then played again to assess the accuracy and quality of the imaged version. The athlete would go through this process about ten to fifteen times in a session. Eventually, it is very likely that the video will become redundant, due to the increased imagery skill of the athlete. However, variety in imagery training is just as important as variety in physical training, so think about using this approach occasionally to supplement your programme.

The imagery fundaMENTALs

● 1. *Mentally warm-up before you carry-out your imagery training session.*

● 2. *Focus on "real-time" imagery, using as many of the senses as possible. Try to create as realistic an image as possible.*

● 3. *Use your natural imagery perspective (internal or external) to begin with. Look to develop both perspectives in time.*

● 4. *When starting your imagery training, set yourself short sessions to be regularly carried out through the week.*

● 5. *Don't compromise the quality of sessions for quantity. If you're losing concentration, stop the session after one more quality image.*

● 6. *Once you have the basic skills, experiment with imagery to find out how it works best for you. Try it before or after physical training. Alter your body position for different sessions, and maybe try using video to enhance the sessions.*

● 7. *Practise imagery regularly, and don't stop once you think you're getting good. The mind is like a muscle — stop training it and it will lose its efficiency.*

Chapter 5
Attentional control: The concentration plan

Every ball is for me the first ball, whether my score is 0 or 200, and I never visualise the possibility of anybody getting me out.

Sir Donald Bradman,
the most successful batsman in cricket history

Concentration is a relaxed state of being alert. Athletes need to be capable of shutting out distractions and paying attention to the things that matter in their sport performance. This is particularly the case at the "critical moments" of performance. It is essential at these times that athletes are completely focused on the necessary cues for successful execution of a skill. We call these cues the "critical cues". Before reading further, we'd like to consider your performance for a moment. What are the critical moments in your sport? What are the critical cues on which you must focus in order to perform with excellence during these moments? And, how good are you at focusing on these cues and blocking out everything else which may act as a distraction? These are the challenges of concentration training and these questions form the basis of an attentional control training programme — a process of improving concentration skills.

Successful performers are able to focus on appropriate thoughts and block out irrelevant distractions.

Concentration is a skill and hence some people are very good at it and others are not. Nevertheless, like all skills, there is always room for improvement — however small it may be. But, improvement will only occur if the skill is practised on a regular basis. This chapter will give you some hints on how you can develop a training programme to improve your concentration skills.

Distractions

Distractions come in two forms. First, athletes get distracted by external factors. These are things which they cannot help paying attention to in the environment but which are not integral to the execution of the task at hand — namely executing a sport skill.

Sample list of external distractions in sport

Noise in the crowd.

The clicking of a camera.

Movement seen in peripheral vision.

Verbal attempts to intimidate by opposition.

Seeing coach or parent get up and leave.

Different sports vary immensely in the type of external distractions which form part of the natural competition setting. For example, many team games consist of large audiences which make a lot of noise. This is potentially very distracting but it must be tolerated as it is an accepted part of the sport. In basketball, opposing supporters seated behind the hoop make furious efforts to distract a player making a free throw attempt by waving their hands, shouting, whistling, holding up banners and jumping up and down. All of these things are visible to the player through peripheral vision but they must be blocked out. In other sports such as golf and snooker, the atmosphere in the audience is completely different. There is an expectation that spectators will remain quiet during performance and consequently the smallest sound such as a camera clicking can be an enormous distraction.

Athletes also frequently lose concentration due to internal distractions. This occurs when the athlete is thinking about something unrelated to the specifics of the task at hand.

Sample list of internal distractions

Thinking about a previous error.

Worrying about the importance of the next point.

Anger at an umpire's poor decision.

Concern about whether injured knee will influence performance.

Getting too analytical about the game.

It is common for athletes to dwell on previous errors or worry too much about the consequences of not winning the next point. These are self-generated thoughts which divert attention from the critical cues discussed earlier. Annoyance at a referee's decision is another typical example of an internal distraction. Although, the referee is an external factor, it is the athlete's emotional reaction to the decision which forms the distraction — rather than the decision itself. The key principle here is that it is an athlete's reaction to a problem which determines whether concentration will be lost — as opposed to the problem itself.

So, the goal of any concentration improvement programme is to minimise the impact of these external and internal distractions and maximise the chances of the athlete focusing intently on the relevant critical cues. Ideally, of course, and during bouts of peak performance athletes don't really think of anything. Performance occurs in an effortless fashion where everything seems to operate automatically. This state of performance has been likened to driving a car. Once an individual has learned the skill of driving (which is extremely complex in the beginning), it is possible to drive in a relaxed, confident state where the various movements involved in changing gear, braking, accelerating and steering take place at the subconscious level. Athletes often report that this is exactly how they felt when they performed at their best. "It just happened" they say. "I didn't have to think about it. It all came so naturally. I was relaxed but highly focused." Well, this is the state of attentional control that we are aiming for during this chapter. That ideal performance state where everything fits into place and it all feels so good.

However, there are two other important factors which cannot be overlooked in any discussion of concentration. They are fatigue and anxiety. Both these factors are known to have detrimental effects on the quality of an athlete's concentration. As far as fatigue is concerned, it's much harder to pay attention to the critical cues when you're tired because it takes more of an effort. This is why silly mistakes so often occur in the latter stages of a competition. Concentration just slips for a few seconds and ...boom....the mistake has been made and a goal has been conceded — perhaps a goal to lose the match.

Anxiety has a different effect on concentration. Many individuals get highly focused when they are anxious and appear totally immersed in what they are doing. Sometimes this is positive but research shows us that a problem known as "attentional narrowing" often arises with excessive anxiety and nerves. This refers to when athletes suffer from inappropriate tunnel vision and fail to pick up on important, perhaps critical, cues from the environment. For example, when passing the ball in a team sport it is easy to miss a lurking defender who can intercept the pass if the athlete is too narrowly focused on the pass receiver. Alternatively, athletes can become so anxious during a performance, and consequently so narrowly focused, that they miss the most obvious cues relating to strategy. For example, we have known squash, tennis and badminton players not realise that their opponent has a very weak backhand until well into the match. This mistake can have serious implications for shot selection and general match strategy and if not observed early enough could be a crucial missed opportunity for gaining a hold on the match.

Before we explain the various training techniques for improving concentration it is well worth considering that an elevated level of fitness and enhanced ability to control anxiety can be straightforward methods which can yield noticeable improvements in concentration. These two changes in readiness will reduce the risk of fatigue influencing concentration and overcome the problem of unwanted attentional narrowing. We suggest that you consult chapter 6 very carefully if you feel that anxiety causes you to narrow your attention inappropriately.

Personal concentration planner

As suggested earlier, the first step in improving concentration involves assessing your sport and your own attentional abilities. So, let's recap on the questions we asked at the beginning of the chapter. First, *what are the critical moments in your sport? When is it absolutely essential that concentration is at it's highest?* There may only be one critical moment or there may be several. When you've identified when these critical moments occur, consider what you need to be focusing on during these moments. Be very precise in this assessment. Perhaps observe world class performers in your sport and take note of what they seem to be focusing on. Again, sports will vary and there may be only one critical cue or there may be several. Finally, evaluate your own attentional abilities. *How good are you at focusing on the critical cues at the critical moments? When does your concentration have a tendency to break down? Are there any specific times when you seem to regularly find it hard to maintain focus?*

When you've accurately answered each of these questions, you have the basis for your personal concentration planner. As you work through the remaining strategies, constantly refer to this planner in guiding your implementation of the techniques described. This will be far more productive than working through the strategies without any specific focus in mind. Your goal should be to use the strategies to maximise concentration at the key times and if you can do this, concentration at other times should fall into place.

Attentional cues

One of the most successful ways of focusing attention on the right things at the right times is to make use of concentration cues. These cues allow athletes to intensify, and relax, concentration voluntarily. They are very individual and must be devised with the nature of the sport, and the attentional style of the athlete, in mind. Three types of concentration cue exist — verbal, visual and physical. A verbal cue is usually a single word which is silently repeated at the appropriate moment. A visual cue involves focusing intently on something very specific in the environment. And a physical cue involves actually doing something behavioural. Examples of each type of cue are shown below:

Examples of concentration cues

VERBAL: *"Focus"*
"Ready"
"Smooth"
"Switch on"
"Head"
"Low"

VISUAL: *Looking at the strings of a tennis racquet*
Focusing briefly on a specific spot on the ground
Staring at the writing on the ball
Looking at a sticker on the back of the hand
Seeing the opponent assume a ready position

PHYSICAL: *Wiping hand on shirt*
Taking a deep breath
Bouncing the ball three times
Tapping the ground with the racquet/stick
Closing eyes momentarily

Some athletes use a single cue whereas others prefer to use a combination. For example, a tennis player may stare at the strings of the racquet, spin the ball in the hand and repeat the word "smooth" at the same time. Whichever cues are chosen, however, they must be practised regularly, and used consistently. If this is done, the cues will eventually become automatic and will operate at the subconscious level. When this is achieved, concentration will not be an effort and performance consistency will improve.

So, think about the three different types of concentration cues — some of which you may use already — and consider how you could use them during performance in your sport. They are particularly useful for assisting athletes in the switching on and off process. Sports which last long periods of time require athletes to vary their level of attentional intensity depending on the state of the game. For example, it is not possible for a baseball player to maintain a high level of concentration for the entire game. So, it is necessary to intensify attentional focus at certain times — usually when the pitcher releases the ball and immediately afterwards. At other times, particularly when the player is sitting on the bench waiting to bat or field, it is appropriate to "rest the mind" and decrease attentional intensity. Concentration cues significantly facilitate this switching on and off process.

Concentration cues can also be helpful for athletes who have a tendency to become distracted by specific things. An international squash player was once taught how to slap the side wall as a reminder to stay calm when a bad decision was made by an official. A table tennis player was taught to stare at a red sticker on the hand as a reminder to stay focused during certain periods of the game where there was a tendency to lose concentration. A soccer player with a tendency to retaliate was taught to take a deep breath and repeat a positive self-affirmation whenever an opposing player attempted a provocative gesture.

Perhaps you can consider any elements in your sport which have a detrimental influence on your concentration. If there are, experiment with the use of a specific cue which you implement every time the distraction occurs.

This, of course, requires considerable practice and patience. Don't expect overnight miracles once you start using a concentration cue. Like any other skill, it will take time before you are comfortable with it and begin to see the performance benefits.

Performance routines

The next progression from the use of concentration cues is the development of performance routines. These routines are very common in sport and can be observed readily by watching successful performers. The baseball pitcher before releasing the ball; the rugby kicker before taking a conversion kick at goal; the tennis player before serving; the long jumper before commencing the run-up; the sprinter before getting set in the blocks; and the golfer before making a putt.

The famous golfer Ray Floyd was well-known for having a very meticulous pre-shot routine — and for being a very tough competitor. During the 1986 US Open he was about to play an approach shot to the 16th hole of the final round. He was holding a slim, one shot lead. As he was about to swing his club, a press photographer distracted him. Floyd backed away from the shot, walked around behind the ball and began his pre-shot routine all over again. The ball landed close to the pin and he held the putt for a birdie going on to win the competition. This was an example of the 'clutch' situation which was described by Simon Barnes at the beginning of this book. Floyd held his nerve in this clutch situation by using a pre-shot routine which prevented the distraction from disrupting his focus of attention.

Research has frequently shown that one of the factors which distinguishes elite from less successful sport performers is the consistency with which the elite athletes approach skill execution. Performance routines are a significant part of this consistency. Club athletes tend to vary their pre-performance behaviours and lack any sort of systematic build-up to skill execution. Consequently, some times things go right and performance is good but much of the time, too much is left to chance and errors occur. Typically, consistency in

My (putting) routine starts when I get the ball back from my caddie after he has cleaned it....I squat and replace the ball in front of my marker, placing the manufacturer's label and the number to the back, where I want to make contact. I walk back and study my intended line. Then I walk forward to the side of the ball and set my putter down behind it, aiming the face down the line I have chosen. I next position my body, probably wriggling my feet a little bit as I get comfortable, aligning myself with the putter face......As I'm getting my body into position, I usually look down my intended line, getting a feel for the speed of the putt and the force I will need in my stroke. I look back down at the ball, focusing on the number on the back. I look down the line one more time. Then I look back at the number, where I want to make contact, and start my stroke ......
Simplistically, that is my routine. Those are the guidelines. You can find the routine that works for you. Maybe you will incorporate a practice stroke or two. Maybe you will take one look or three or four looks. Whatever, you choose to do, ingrain it into your system so you do the same things the same way every time.

Ray Floyd,
former champion golfer

pre-performance routine is often lost when things are not going well and athletes are losing. Ironically, this is usually the very time when the need for consistency and stability is at its highest.

Performance routines work for three main reasons. First, they help the athlete block out irrelevant internal and external distractions by providing something on which to focus. Second, they assist in the general calming process. They provide a sense of familiarity which facilitates in the process of reminding that it's just another shot, another serve, or another race. In turn, this enhances confidence. Third, by providing a totally consistent pre-performance set of behaviours, the chances of a subsequent consistent performance are maximised. In other words, the routine is setting a scene of stability which provides a solid framework on which to execute the skill.

Routines must be carefully planned and then practised extensively in training before being implemented in competition. Different types of routines exist. The pre-performance routine is the most common but in some sports there are other occasions when a set routine is appropriate.

For example, in tennis, the between-points routine is very important. We know that top tennis players have consistent mannerisms and behaviours in which they engage between points but club players tend to be very erratic in what they do. American sport psychologist Jim Loehr developed the "16 second cure" for tennis players. It was a sequence of behaviours (lasting about 16 seconds) for the player to execute between points. It consisted of placing the racquet in the non-playing hand and relaxing the dominant arm; a little pacing around the baseline; deep breaths and positive imagery. The key to the routine was that it should be implemented between all points regardless of the state of the match. We have successfully implemented variations of this technique with many players and found that it enables them to feel more in control and approach the next point with confidence as well as enhanced levels of concentration.

A post-performance routine is also appropriate in some sports. This is a set of behaviours enabling athletes to review the previous skill execution, learn from it, and then initiate the next element of performance. Sports like archery, bowling and shooting lend themselves to this sort of routine where there is a desire to repeat a skill execution on successive multiple occasions. A three-step performance routine which could be applied to many different sporting situations is shown in the chart below. Examine the routine and then consider how you could adapt it to your own sport performance.

Sample performance routine

Step 1: PREPARATION PHASE
- Step back and carry out a physical cue to tune in attention.
- Take two deep breaths and relax the shoulders and arms.

Step 2: FOCUSING PHASE
- Approach and take one more deep breath.
- Focus the eyes on an appropriate visual cue.
- Visualise successful performance of the skill — feel the movements.

Step 3: EXECUTION PHASE
- Silently repeat a positive verbal cue.
- PERFORM.

On the following page, more specific routines are shown for a tennis serve, putt in golf and a penalty kick in soccer. These may give you further ideas on how to modify the generalised routine for your own needs. When you have devised your routine (or routines), take them to training and practise them over and over again until they become an integral part of your performance. Then you are ready to use them in the competitive situation.

EXAMPLE PERFORMANCE ROUTINES

	TENNIS SERVE	GOLF PUTT	SOCCER PENALTY KICK
Preparation phase	• Adjust racquet strings • Select ball • Deep breath	• Place ball and pick up marker • Assess line and length • Deep breath	• Place ball on spot • Take 3 steps back • Deep breath
Focusing phase	• Approach base line and position feet • Bounce ball 3 times • Pause and focus on target area • Visualise successful serve	• Stand over putt • Focus on line • Visualise successful putt • One practice swing	• Focus on ball • Visualise successful shot • Deep breath • Shoulder relax
Execution phase	• Repeat cue word, e.g., "reach" • Toss ball and serve	• Repeat cue word, e.g., "smooth" • Swing club	• Repeat cue word, e.g., "power" • Take penalty

NOTES:
- Be totally consistent on each performance and stick to the routine
- Practise the routine in training

PERSONAL PERFORMANCE ROUTINE

Preparation phase:

-

-

-

Focusing phase:

-

-

-

-

Execution phase:

-

-

NOTES:
- Completing all the blank lines is not essential
- Be totally consistent on each performance and stick to the routine
- Practise the routine in training

Error parking

Parking is a useful technique for athletes who find it difficult to get errors out of their mind and consequently become distracted by dwelling on them. In simple terms, when using the skill of parking, the athlete creates an image in the mind which successfully removes the distraction and parks it somewhere away from attention in the here and now. The key to the effectiveness of parking, is to find a mental image which has personal meaning to the athlete. Examples of individual parking images which athletes (with whom we have worked) have used in the past are illustrated below.

Examples of personal parking images

- *An international rower saw errors as stones which disappeared when tossed over the side.*

- *A non-smoking Olympic wrestler saw errors as cigarette butts to be fiercely stamped out with his foot.*

- *A university volleyball team imagined errors as garbage. When an error was made on court someone would shout out "chuck it out".*

- *A professional golfer imagined errors being put in a file, placed in a filing cabinet and the drawer being closed.*

The skill of parking errors is particularly dependent on practice. With practice, the athlete establishes an automatic link between the parking image and focusing attention on relevant performance cues. So, the following process must be followed to facilitate use of the skill:

1. Establish an appropriate parking image which has personal meaning and can be comfortably used.
2. Spend time away from training rehearsing the images involved.

3. Practise the skill in a relaxed state during training in order to develop a degree competence and familiarity.

4. Practise the skill in pressurised training situations.

5. Implement the skill in competition.

Simulated practice

Simulated practice is an excellent concentration strategy because it replicates the kind of distracting situations athletes find themselves in during competition. Then, by repeated exposure to these situations during training the athlete becomes desensitised to the distractions and learns to stay focused. We have identified four different types of simulated practice:

● 1 'General noise' training

The world and Olympic archery champion Darrell Pace explained how he used to practise by the side of a busy road or with loud distracting music.

Basketball teams and volleyball teams have trained in sports halls with no spectators but with loud crowd noise being played over the public address system. Then, when they arrive at the competition site to be greeted by spectator noise they are not so affected by it as they would be had they had no practice. This may be particularly useful for inexperienced players who have had limited exposure to playing in front of large crowds.

> **Through the mental training I have developed an intense amount of mental concentration......When I was 16, I would practice at a park where there was nothing around, I would set out my car speakers and listen to rock and roll music......I shot by railroad tracks, had cars driving by etc., to practice dealing with distractions. I had to learn to block everything out.**
>
> ***Darrell Pace**, Winner of 3 Olympic archery medals and a world record holder*

● 2 'Sledging' training

The term sledging refers to the delivery of unsporting verbal insults to opposing players in an attempt to unnerve them. The practice occurs in many sports in various forms and can be quite disrupting to the inexperienced performer. So, artificial sledging practice can be created whereby team-mates stand near an athlete during performance practice and play the role of the opposing team by making unwelcome personal comments. Once the strange feeling of this artificial situation has been overcome, it can be a very useful exercise in developing the ability to block out these kind of comments and focus on performing the skill in question.

● 3 'Poor official' training

Poor decisions by officials are very distracting to many athletes and can disrupt the whole momentum of performance. One bad call has frequently led to an athlete losing concentration at a critical time and this inevitably can have disastrous effects on the competition outcome. Athletes must learn to accept the decisions of officials, whether they agree with them or not. To assist in this process, we have collaborated with coaches to contrive a practice game situation whereby a mock official is told to purposely make bad calls or perhaps favour one athlete or team. Provided this is done skilfully, it can be very effective at desensitising athletes to bad decisions. Athletes have to learn how to control their reactions and stay focused on their performance. They must focus on "controlling the controllables" rather than getting upset by factors over which they have no influence. The best way to develop this concentration skill is to practise it — again, and again, and again.

● 4 'Bad luck' training

Bad luck can disrupt concentration very quickly sometimes. However, sport is all about luck. In fact, dictionary definitions usually identify the role of fortune as being an integral part of "sport". The bounce of the ball, weather conditions, and equipment failure are three of the most common elements of luck which play a significant part in the outcome of competition. To desensitise athletes to the impact of bad luck on performance we have used conditioned practice situations where athletes are given a piece of bad luck to play with in training. Examples of this are listed at the foot of this page.

By practising under these unfavourable conditions, we have found that athletes develop their mental toughness and are able to stay focused on the critical cues as opposed to moaning and whining about how "it's not fair". In fact, we find that the tougher athletes even start to relish the challenge of competing successfully when the odds are against them and really concentrate intently on overcoming the bad luck they have been dealt.

We suggest you review the examples below and then consider any bad luck training situations you could practise as part of your training. Obviously a coach would be able to assist you in this process and perhaps your team-mates may also have some good ideas.

Examples of 'bad luck' conditions for practice

Tennis player having to play against an opponent who is allowed to make three cheating line calls per practice set.

Soccer team which must play with one player short (simulating a sending off).

Golfer whose lie is worsened on every third hole.

Hockey team which must begin practice match two goals down.

Gymnast whose floor exercise music stops after 15 seconds.

Sprinter who gets into the blocks and then must get up and prepare all over again (twice!).

Basketball team players who are regularly, but incorrectly, called for a travelling offence.

Concentration imagery training

In chapter 4 we introduced you to the skill of imagery. You can use imagery specifically to enhance concentration skill in two main ways. First, by visualising successful performance in the situations which are most distracting. Visualise yourself coping with the distractions and performing with excellence despite the attentional difficulties of the situation. Second, imagery can be done with the use of an audio-tape containing distracting sounds such as crowd noise.

Whilst carrying out this imagery rehearsal it is useful if you combine the images with positive self-talk. "I can concentrate really well" or "Distractions bring out the best in my mental toughness" are examples of self-statements which could usefully accompany concentration imagery.

As usual though, if imagery is to have a noticeable effect on concentration skill, it must be practised regularly — several times per week for short periods of several minutes.

Inner game training

In the 1970s Timothy Gallwey introduced the world of sport to the "inner game" approach. This approach encouraged athletes to relax and play sport almost by instinct rather than by analysis. It is true that many athletes do not perform well because, in trying to concentrate, they experience "paralysis by analysis". They over-analyse and become obsessive about their technique and its execution. As a result, their performance becomes forced and unnatural. Gallwey discussed the need to develop the skill of relaxed concentration and he claimed that the secret of winning in sport lies in not trying too hard. He discussed the ongoing battle between "Self 1" and "Self 2". Self 1 refers to the part of the mind which gives instructions and attempts to solve problems analytically. Self 2 refers to the part of the mind which allows us to be intuitive and act automatically. By discovering these two selves and then using them appropriately, Gallwey has helped many athletes, at all levels, to improve their performance. In particular, the inner game seems to work well in the sports of tennis, golf and skiing.

So, to develop your inner game approach you need to avoid getting too analytical about your performance. Relax and let it happen. Go with your feelings and enjoy your performance. Forget the coaching manuals and rely on your automatic responses. The results may surprise you!

The concentration fundaMENTALs

● 1. *Identify the specific attentional demands of your sport and the particular distractions which are most likely to disrupt your performance.*

● 2. *Use concentration cues to focus attention on appropriate things at the critical moments.*

● 3. *Develop performance routines and practise them in training.*

● 4. *Experiment with the skill of parking as a means of dealing with errors and other internal distractions.*

● 5. *Use various simulated practice techniques to desensitise yourself to the effects of external distractions.*

● 6. *Practise concentrating by using visualisation.*

● 7. *Relax and let things happen automatically.*

Chapter 6
Anxiety control: The arousal management plan

I discovered that after a certain point of nervousness, I would start to deteriorate pretty rapidly. There was real drop-off point in my ability to perform if I got too nervous.... So it was just being able to find that little narrow comfort zone.

Steve Podborski,
former World Cup Downhill ski champion

Athletes like a certain amount of stress in their sporting lives. Indeed, the pressure of competition is one of the things which many athletes find exhilarating and motivating. However, too much stress is known to influence performance negatively and if an athlete is not capable of managing excessive levels of stress, then successful performance on "the big days" will be very elusive.

The ideal performance state of an athlete is one in which there is a feeling of being really 'psyched' and ready for competition. Without mental skills for managing arousal, this is a very difficult thing to achieve on a consistent basis. To be at one's optimal level of arousal for each performance takes skill. It doesn't just happen. So, acquiring the appropriate skills for voluntarily controlling unwanted anxiety and arousal is an important part of developing your mental game plan. These skills will enable you to reduce arousal levels when you're feeling over-anxious and to increase arousal when you're not feeling pumped up enough.

The role of anxiety

It is widely accepted that the relationship between perform-ance and arousal results from the interaction of two types of anxiety. Technically, these two types of anxiety are referred to as cognitive and somatic. Cognitive anxiety results from ap-prehensions and concerns we have about the demands of the situation. This is characterised by feelings of worry, lack of confidence and inability to concentrate. Typically, athletes experience el-evated levels of cognitive anxiety well before the start of a competi-tion. In some cases many days in advance. Somatic anxiety, on the other hand, results from how we interpret the physiological reac-tions in our bodies. Our acknowl-edgement of things like butterflies, muscle tension, sweaty palms and increased heart rate are all signs of somatic anxiety. Typically, somatic anxiety levels are elevated much closer to the start of the competition and often disappear soon after performance is underway.

> **Strange, but I didn't feel as nervous as I thought I would. Perhaps that was the trouble.**
>
> *Rob Andrew, speaking about the Grand Slam defeat by Scotland in 1990*

In basic terms then, these two types of anxiety can be categorised as "mental" and "physical". We'll refer to them in this way for the rest of this chapter. But more importantly, we'll use the term arousal to represent the result of the two types of anxiety interacting and producing a state of emo-tional readiness. One end of the arousal scale is illustrated by an athlete who is highly charged and psyched up — perhaps even aggressive. The other end of the scale is seen in the ath-lete who is very relaxed and calm.

The sports arousal scale

The relationship between mental and physical anxiety is, in fact, quite complex. This complexity comes from the fact that there are no absolute levels of arousal which are optimal for all athletes performing in all sports. Rather, both individuals and sports require distinctly different levels of arousal in order for optimum performance to occur. Contrast the arousal required by an American football linebacker with that needed by a golfer attempting to sink a putt for the match on the 18th green. Likewise, even athletes within the same sport, doing the same job, vary in the ideal level of arousal they need in order to perform at their best. We're sure you can identify some athletes you know who need to be highly charged before competition and others who need to be much more relaxed and calm. So, your first challenge is to start to think about your own ideal performance state in terms of this arousal level scale. Where do you sit on the pumped up/totally calm continuum? It is not possible to devise your coping strategies for inappropriate pre-competitive arousal before answering this question. And of course, the answer may vary according to the type of competition or the nature of the opposition.

> **Being nervous isn't a problem as long as I can control it and make it work for me. Anxiety affects me in two ways - physically and mentally. It's hard to maintain the physical relaxation needed to play flowing rhythmical strokes when I'm over-anxious, and this can lead to technical faults. My timing comes from having my head and weight over the ball while playing the shot, but when I get too nervous I tense up and start pushing stiffly too early at the ball and end up either hitting it in the air or flashing at it outside the off stump.**
>
> *Robin Smith, international cricketer*

You may need to vary your arousal levels at will on a regular basis. You can now appreciate why arousal management is such an important mental training skill for an athlete to practise.

The ideal 'Zone'

It is thought that athletes actually have a band of arousal levels within which they perform their best. If the athlete is above or below this band, performance deteriorates. The band within which best performances occur is known as the 'zone of optimal functioning' or the 'zone' for short. When an athlete is in the 'zone', optimal performances are most likely to occur. So, we feel that it is very important for athletes to be able to identify the signs and symptoms which indicate being 'in zone'. The importance of being able to 'read one's body' becomes even more clear when you consider the interactive process of mental and physical anxiety and the resulting relationship with performance.

Have you ever been in the situation where everything is going really well, your performance level is great and then suddenly nothing can seem to go right? It's as if your performance fell off a cliff. Well, in fact that may just be what happened. In the past it was thought that the relationship between performance and arousal was like an inverted U curve. As arousal increased gradually, so did performance up to a point. And then as

> Never have I seen more pent-up fury, more raw emotion, than there was before kick-off that day... It was all too much for Dean Richards, a product of the silent and contemplative school of self-motivation, who walked out of the changing room. Each to his own. Richards produced yet another colossal performance on the field that day.
>
> *Rob Andrew,*
> *former rugby*
> *international*

arousal continued to increase, performance gradually de-creased. It was thought that you could move performance back up this down slope by gradually decreasing arousal. However, more recent sport psychology research evidence has questioned this belief and supported what most athletes have experienced — the sudden, and major, decrease in perform-ance. The falling off the performance cliff. The new evidence also supports the view that performance does not go back up gradually after one of these major drops but that the athlete requires a major calm down before performance begins to im-prove again. This new research identifies an even greater need for athletes to get their arousal levels right prior to, and dur-ing, competition. If not, it is extremely difficult to get back into the zone — especially if arousal management skills have not been mastered.

Athlete reversals

As we have said, anxiety affects athletes in different ways. Re-versal theory suggests that these differences in interpretation may result from the way performers approach situations. If an athlete approaches a situation with feelings of being serious-minded, and focuses too much on performance outcome, then increases in arousal are interpreted as negative and lead to feelings of stress. This athlete would not enjoy the high pres-sure of competition. He/she would interpret low arousal posi-tively, leading to feelings of being relaxed and happy. The re-verse type of athlete approaches competitions by focusing simply on enjoying the sensations of participating, and aiming to achieve performance potential. Increases in arousal are interpreted by this type of athlete as exciting, and exhilarating. These athletes therefore enjoy the feelings of high-pressure competition so much. With this approach to competition low arousal levels usually lead athletes to report feelings of rest-lessness and boredom. Most people will have one approach which they usually find themselves taking for competition, but from time to time they reverse into the opposite approach. This might help to explain why different performers react differently to the pressure of competition, and why on some days we react completely differently than on other days. Try

> During one Ashes tour he (Ian Botham) spent the entire time playing cribbage in the bowels of the dressing room until it was his turn to bat. This was not out of indiffer–ence, it was an attempt to escape from the tension and the momentous expectations every time he entered the arena. Even Botham could be very nervous.
>
> *Vic Marks*,
> *former cricketer and now media correspondent*

and work out if you have one typical approach to competition.

Strategies for managing anxiety and arousal

It is generally felt that mental anxiety is usually a hindrance to performance and needs to be decreased. Physical anxiety, on the other hand, and particularly in some sports, can be quite useful within manageable levels. So there may be occasions when pumping up instead of calming down is necessary. Many sport psychologists suggest that the technique for reducing excessive anxiety should be matched with the type of anxiety being experienced. In other words, mental anxiety requires a mental strategy whereas physical anxiety requires a physical strategy.

This makes sense and so we have adopted this approach in this chapter. We first identify a number of strategies appropriate for dealing with mental anxiety and then a different set of strategies for dealing with physical anxiety. It must be remembered, however, that all individuals differ. And there is always an exception to the rule. It may be that there could be a crossover in these techniques and that a mentally based strategy might successfully deal with physical anxiety or vice versa. We encourage you to keep an open mind. The final section identifies strategies which may be used to 'pump up' or energise if arousal is too low.

So here are our ten top tips for developing an arousal management strategy into your mental game plan. The first two strategies are designed for preparation. Strategies 3, 4 and 5 are designed for reducing mental anxiety. Strategies 6, 7 and 8 are designed for reducing physical anxiety. And finally strategies 9 and 10 are designed for 'pumping arousal up' when necessary. Developing a plan which utilises these strategies where appropriate will maximise your chances of getting psyched for performance by being in "the zone".

> **You're only here for a short visit, so don't hurry, don't worry, and be sure to stop and smell the flowers along the way.**
>
> *Walter Hagen, former golf champion*

Ten top tips for managing sports arousal

● *1 Ideal performance state awareness*

It is crucial that athletes understand the arousal levels within which they perform their best. Often, this is a trial-and-error process, but the process can be enhanced by paying careful attention to pre-competition feelings and subsequent performance. Athletes often observe a consistent relationship between levels of arousal and performance which may be contrary to what they had expected. Many may have never considered whether their pre-competition arousal level is actually appropriate. Many athletes habitually 'over-psych' themselves without realising how detrimental over-arousal can be. The quotation by Rob Andrew earlier in the chapter (p. 108) illustrates how Dean Richards developed his own style of quiet preparation for international rugby matches. Traditionally, rugby has been viewed as a sport requiring excessive levels of pre-competition arousal. Recently, however, more and more coaches and players have become aware that players vary significantly in their ideal performance states.

● *2 Pre-competition arousal check*

As part of your pre-competition routine (a skill we discuss in more detail throughout chapter 9), you should have a built-in arousal check. This is a simple technique which encourages you to pause for a few moments and read your body/mind signals. During this period, you ask yourself whether your level of arousal is appropriate. Are you in the 'zone'? If not, you need to implement one, or some, of the techniques described below in order to alter your arousal to a desirable level in order to facilitate the ideal performance state. It's important that your arousal check is long enough before the start of competition to give you time to implement any changes. However, the check must not be too long before competition begins or else arousal level could be altered again and fall outside the desirable zone. Getting this timing right will perhaps take a while but talking with more experienced athletes and coaches may help in the early stages. Finally, the check should include a monitoring of how you're thinking as well as feeling. It may be that one type of anxiety needs attention whereas the other can be left alone.

● *3 Appraisal changing*

When athletes experience elevated levels of mental anxiety, they are usually worrying about three things. First, they worry about the demands of the situation. Second, they worry about their ability to cope with these demands. And third, they worry about the consequences of not meeting the demands of the situation. Examples of each of these three worries are shown in the list opposite.

This type of negative thinking inevitably results in anxiety and usually in poor performance. One of the most consistent findings in sport psychology research over the past twenty five years is the direct relationship between positive thinking and successful performance. You have already been introduced to this area in chapter 3, and much of that material can be applied in the current context of anxiety reduction. You need to train yourself to be more confident by practising positive self-talk on a regular basis. Part of your mental train-

Typical worries of athletes which cause mental anxiety

Demand worries

"This is a really tough course."

"The opposition is the best in the league. They're unbeaten this season."

"The TV cameras are here — no one told me. That's all I need!"

Ability worries

"I've never played in front of so many people. What if I choke?"

"There's no way we can deal with their offence — it's unstoppable."

"I just can't see myself pulling it off today."

Consequence worries

"If I don't perform well today, I know I'll be dropped from the squad."

"My coach will be so disappointed if I fail. She's given up so much of her time."

"I could kill myself on that course!"

ing should be consistent repetition of specific positive self-statements. You can do this while your travelling on a train, while you're lying in the bath or when you dropping off to sleep. But the principle is that you are training your mind to think positively as a natural response to challenge. If you can do this successively, you'll begin to change the mental anxiety into feelings of challenge and excitement.

So, as far as the three types of worry are concerned, you need to re-appraise the situation with a positive frame of mind. The list below provides examples of how you can re-appraise your thinking in each of the three areas. Compare the different tones of this and the previous list.. You can see how anxiety can be reduced by the appropriate form of appraisal and thinking.

Coping self-talk to reduce mental anxiety

Demands

"Although this course is tough, I know I've done the necessary preparation."

"This team has to lose sometime — today could be the day."

"TV cameras don't change the challenge of this match — it's still the same game."

Ability

"These people are here to enjoy the game — let's give them something to watch."

"They have a great offence so let's make sure we stick to our game plan — it can work."

"Stick to the basics and relax. Do what you do best."

Consequences

"Forget the future for now. Just think about my job today."

"I'm performing for me — don't worry what others will think."

"Control the controllables — that's as much as I can do."

Reducing competitive anxiety by keeping things in perspective

A sense of perspective. After a decade of high level rugby, I'm convinced that this is the secret to long and contented survival in the often neurotic and obsessive world of sport.

Rob Andrew, former rugby international

Judo is not the most important thing in my life — but sometimes it has to feel like it.....Really, how can you say a sport is the most important thing in life? I just have to train as if it was.

Nicola Fairbrother, World Lightweight Judo Champion

There is a further antidote to nerves, which is to realise that no golf shot is a matter of life or death.

Ray Floyd, former golf champion

All you can do Kate is be your best and let the results take care of themselves. Be YOUR best — not necessarily the WORLD'S best. It's just another race, another start gate, another start hut—and me.

Kate Pace, 1993 World Downhill Ski Champion, describing her pre-race self-talk

It's not the end of the world. My dog will still lick my face whether I win or lose.

Matt Biondi, US swimmer, after losing his Olympic title in 1992

I haven't lost a war. No one got killed. I just lost a tennis match.

Boris Becker, German tennis player, after losing in the second round at Wimbledon, as defending champion, 1987

Sure it was important to me, but to who else? The sun will be out tomorrow and the stars and the moon will be out tonight. It was only a race.

Michael Johnson, US sprinter after failing to qualify for the Olympic 200 meters final in 1992 when he was favourite to win the event

Sometimes I lie in bed at night and think, 'I jump into a sandpit for a living. Am I doing anything worthwhile here? The pointlessness of it.' You see doctors in Rwanda and think, 'They are making a difference, but I am jumping into a sandpit'.

Jonathan Edwards, World Champion triple jumper

● *4 Imagery*

Again, the skill of imagery has been dealt with earlier in the book but it is also an effective strategy for coping with mental anxiety. Recalling previous good performances and seeing future success have been shown to be extremely effective for some athletes. So, re-read the chapter and look again at how you may use this important skill. As with all the mental skills, you will need to practise it on a regular basis so that your images are clear and controllable.

Then, when anxiety becomes a problem in the period preceding competition, you can find a quiet place and do some positive imagery where you see yourself performing well and coping with the challenges which will be thrown at you. If finding a quiet place is a problem prior to competition, you can always lock yourself in the loo and use the toilet as a seat. This has been done many times before although athletes may not be prepared to admit it! So don't feel silly or embarrassed. If you need time alone to collect your thoughts and do some imagery — you've got to find somewhere!

> I coped with stress by playing cards, getting totally involved in a book, or retreating to a quiet place on my own.
>
> **Shane Gould**, *former Olympic swimming champion*

● *5 Focused breathing*

If you don't have much time to reduce physical anxiety then taking a few deep breaths is a tried and tested technique which works for most people. Focusing on relaxation in the fingertips and toes is a quick method of instilling whole body relaxation.

A very simple five-step version of this technique is shown on the opposite page.

A focused breathing routine

Step 1:   Find a place where you can sit down and will not be pushed or moved.

Step 2:   Breathe deeply in through the nose and out through the mouth according to the following routine:

Inhale through nose: Count IN, TWO THREE, FOUR.

Exhale through mouth: Count OUT, TWO THREE, FOUR.

Focus: on relaxed fingertips.

Step 3:   Breathe deeply in through the nose and out through the mouth according to the following routine:

Inhale through nose: Count IN, TWO THREE, FOUR.

Exhale through mouth: Count OUT, TWO THREE, FOUR.

Focus: on relaxed toes.

Step 4:   Repeat this breathing process as many times as you are able or as many times as you need.

Step 5:   Stand up and silently repeat "I feel ready — I feel good."

This breathing routine will be most effective if it has been practised regularly during training and the athlete is comfortable and familiar with the exercise. Don't expect the routine to work on your first attempt. Experiment with its use. Try it at different times. Get used to the feelings associated with getting control of your physical anxiety. And then you'll find it will work in the pre-competition period. A shortened version of this breathing routine can, of course, be used during performance. Experienced athletes find that they can pause, take one long deep breath and refocus very effectively during a break in performance. This comes with a great deal of practice, however, but is an extremely useful arousal control technique to have up your sleeve.

● *6 Deep relaxation training*

Although not a technique that is recommended for use immediately prior to competition, deep relaxation is an effective way of reducing physical anxiety in the days leading up to competition. It is also a very useful way of recovering from a hard training session as well as generally reducing the physical effects of stress. We've devised a 10 step version of this exercise routine which is described below, but we would encourage you to adapt our version to suit your own preferences.

Deep relaxation is a very individual experience and athletes vary enormously in what works for them in terms of inducing a really relaxed state. So be prepared to experiment and add in your own elements to the routine if you find that helps.

The 10 step deep relaxation routine

Step 1:   Find a place where you can lie down or sit down comfortably with your head supported.

Step 2:   Put on some music which you find really relaxing — a personal stereo is very useful.

Step 3:   Close your eyes and then spend a couple of minutes getting really comfortable and tuning in to your body.

Step 4:   Now focus on your breathing rhythm. Take 10 deep breaths to establish a slow, steady breathing rhythm. Each time you breath out, feel more relaxed and feel some tension begin to disappear.

Step 5: When you feel ready, focus on your right arm. Clench your fist tightly, count to 10, and then slowly open out your fingers and relax your hand and arm completely. Feel your arm go heavy and sink into the floor or chair. Repeat this process once. Then run through the same process for your left arm.

Step 6: Now focus on your right leg. Tighten the muscles in your leg, count to 10, and then relax all the muscles completely. Feel your leg go heavy and try to achieve a sinking feeling. Repeat this process once. Then run through the same process for your left leg.

Step 7: Turn your attention to your face, neck and shoulders. Relax all the muscles in this area and in particular focus on smoothing out the muscles in your forehead. Relax your cheeks, your neck and the back of your shoulders.

Step 8: Focus on relaxing your whole body by concentrating on a relaxed feeling in your fingertips, toes and forehead.

Step 9: Spend several minutes listening to your music, enjoying this relaxed feeling and imagining yourself in a place where you can feel completely relaxed and at ease. This may be on the beach, by a swimming pool, on a boat, in a forest, up a mountain, etc. etc..

Step 10: Count down silently, and slowly, from 10 to 1. As you do so, bend and stretch your arms, move your head from side to side and gradually bring yourself back. As you get to number one, you can open your eyes and tell yourself that you feel relaxed, rested and refreshed.

As you begin to improve your ability to relax deeply using this technique, you'll probably find that your capacity to control arousal before and during competition improves — perhaps using the focused breathing technique. Generally, you will improve your ability to read your body. You will notice the difference between tension and relaxation more easily. And you will be able to manipulate arousal voluntarily far better than you were before.

Hopefully, you will also find the exercise enjoyable. Most of us like a time to ourselves when we can float away and leave our daily hassles behind. Deep relaxation training is your chance to do this on a regular basis.

● *7 Re-interpret feelings*

Sometimes it is very difficult to get rid of the feelings associated with physical anxiety and the resulting arousal. It is therefore useful to reinterpret these feelings in a more positive frame of mind. Rather than interpreting the physical symptoms as negative and potentially harmful to performance, interpret them as a sign of readiness and eagerness to compete. Think about the feelings as excitement about the challenges ahead and in terms of being psyched to do your best under pressure. As the saying goes:

> *"Butterflies are not a problem.*
> *It's just a case of getting them to fly in formation."*

By interpreting your butterflies, increased heart rate and nervous energy as part of your readiness to compete, you can begin to accept these symptoms as useful. Combining this approach with appropriate self-talk and appraisal thoughts will assist in your efforts to achieve the ideal performance state. This technique may not work for all athletes all of the time but it's worth trying in certain situations.

● *8 Inspirational music*

Many athletes find that music is very effective for a pre-competition pump up. The selection of the music is important and very individual. Three different types of music seem to be effective for this use. The first is music which is obviously

**Michael Johnson, relaxing and focusing,
before finally getting settled in the blocks.**

associated with sports perform-ance. Typical examples of this are movie themes such as Chariots of Fire or Rocky. Many athletes report how inspirational these tunes are and play them on their personal stereo as part of their pre-competi-tion preparation.

Patriotic music has also been reported by elite athletes to be effective. School or university songs, national anthems or other obviously nationalistic tunes have been used with great success by athletes in both team, and indi-vidual, sports.

The third type of music is upbeat with some sort of mean-ingful lyrics. Earlier in the book, we mentioned how the England Women's Cricket Team adopted Tina Turner's "Simply the best" as their theme tune for the 1993 World Cup. The England Netball Team took the same song as their theme for the 1995 World Championships. Another popular choice is "We are the champions" by the rock group Queen.

So, we suggest that you con-sider whether there is any music which may have inspirational potential for you. If you can find a suitable piece then keep it in your kit bag and be ready to use it if necessary as a means of psyching up for competition.

> **The night before a competition I listen to a tape on my Walkman. I did that at the Olympics too. There are a couple of songs that really psych me up. The beat goes with my stroke. I can see myself swimming with it, I can feel my stroke and I sort of get excited.**
>
> *Anne Ottenbrite, Olympic swimming champion*

● *9 Physical exertion*

When athletes are feeling lethargic and need pumping up, some sort of physical exertion can work very quickly. Running a few sprints, pushing some weights, or simply running on the spot and breathing vigorously serve to activate the body and mind. Heart rate and respiration rate will increase, and there will be a general feeling of being more energised. In turn, this may serve to enhance psychological activation and assist the athlete in entering the "zone" and achieving the ideal performance state.

● *10 Activating cues*

Some athletes thrive on pressure and actually get nervous if they're not feeling a little anxious. For these athletes, activating cues may be a partial solution when they need energising. The use of cue words or phrases, if appropriately selected, can effectively increase arousal and assist the athlete in entering the 'zone'. A variety of these sorts of cue is shown below. If this strategy appeals to you, we suggest that you experiment with different cues to see which ones work most effectively for you.

Examples of activating cues

"Come on — let's go."

"This is the big one — let's hit it."

"The pressure's on today — this is what I love."

"I need to be hot today — let's really focus."

"I love pressure".

"Drive hard — attack early."

"This is tough competition — I'm really psyched".

The sports arousal management fundaMENTALs

1. Build an arousal check into your competition preparation routine.

2. Change the way you think about competition and focus on positive self-talk.

3. Use imagery to see yourself performing well in pressure situations.

4. Develop the skills of focused breathing and deep relaxation for use at appropriate times.

5. Think of butterflies and nerves as your body being ready for competition.

6. Use inspirational music, physical exertion and activating thoughts when you need to increase arousal.

Chapter 7
Injury:
The recovery plan

I wouldn't wish injury on anyone, but you don't really know what the game's all about until you've experienced it.

Steve Backley,
British world record javelin thrower

It happens!

Eight out of every ten athletes who have a career lasting more than five years are likely to get injured at some time. Sport breeds injury very readily. The increase in sports injury clinics and physiotherapists specialising in the rehabilitation of athletes indicate the improvement in medical services now available for the diagnosis and treatment of athletic ailments. However, the psychology of sports injury is an area which has begun to interest researchers and it is now acknowledged that mental training skills can be a very useful tool for the injured athlete. Indeed, many sport psychologists claim that the management of injury is just another sports skill.

There are three different aspects of psychology relating to sports injury. First, the athlete's emotional reaction to getting injured. Second, the factors which influence the extent to which the athlete does what the physiotherapist recommends in terms of injury rehabilitation. And third, the various mental skills which can be used to maintain a positive attitude during the recovery period. Each of these aspects will be dealt with separately during the remainder of this chapter.

Reactions to getting injured

Some experts suggest that when athletes get injured, they can experience similar emotions to those described by Elizabeth Kubler-Ross of an individual responding to a life event which causes a grief response. In fact, it appears that many athletes pass through different emotional phases which bear close resemblance to those of the grieving individual. These phases are shown oppospite. The emotions described in this table are often complicated by athletes feeling abandoned and alone when they get injured. Athletes frequently report a sense of isolation following injury due to their being excluded from training and even team meetings. It is common for coaches and administrators to lose interest in injured athletes. The extreme case of this is where an injured athlete is actively encouraged to stay away from the rest of the squad due to a concern that the injury may have a demoralising effect on other athletes.

During the transition through these reaction phases, athletes must also often have to cope with pain, insomnia and boredom.

The challenge for those individuals supporting injured athletes is to help them through these reaction phases as smoothly as possible. The intention should not be to miss phases out but to speed up the transition process so that the athlete is looking ahead with optimism as soon as is realistically possible.

So, our recommendation is that athletes should be given permission to go through the anger and depression phases. These are perfectly natural responses to a situation which has such significance to them. But, we discourage athletes from dwelling on these emotions for too long. Moving forward to the final two phases is very important if positive psychological adjustment to the injury is to take place. This is where a positive, mentally tough attitude will be very useful.

Phases of reaction to a sports injury

Phase	*Typical athlete reactions*
DENIAL	*"It's all right, it's nothing."* *"I'll be OK after I've stretched a bit."* *"There's no problem, I can play through it."* *"Don't worry about me, I'm fine."*
ANGER AND FRUSTRATION	*"*********!! My hamstring's gone."* *"Now I'll miss the big cup match."* *"I'll be after that defender next year."*
DEPRESSION	*"Why me?"* *"Why now?"* *"I'll never get another chance?"* *"It's not fair — why did it have to happen one week before the trials?"* *"I can't play for three months."*
ACKNOWLEDGE-MENT AND ACCEPTANCE	*"OK, so it's happened, I've got to accept it."* *"Getting injured is part of sport."* *"It could be worse — at least I'm not out for the season."*
HOPE AND FUTURE PLANNING	*"I'll be back and I'll be stronger than ever."* *"Let's meet with the coach and set my recovery goals."* *"I'll use this recovery time to work on my imagery skills."*

Kate Pace, a fine example of a mentally tough athlete (as we have already illustrated earlier in the book) used to cope with the negative emotions associated with injury recovery by thinking extremely positively. She experienced a number of significant injuries during her career before becoming World Champion but used the phrase "climbing on adversity" to help her cope. She would tell herself that the injury experience would make her tougher and stronger. She would make a commitment to win the first race in which she competed after her rehabilitation. And she imagined her skiing career in the form of a staircase — viewing herself as staying on the same stair when she got injured rather than slipping backwards. Each time she got injured, she viewed herself as pausing that much higher on the staircase.

These positive feelings and thoughts are excellent examples for other athletes to follow.

Sticking with a rehabilitation programme

The research on British athletes of Dr Adrian Taylor and Dr Sally May has recently shown that 50% of injured athletes do not comply with the recommendations of their physiotherapist. This figure is irrespective of performance level and relates to athletes not resting properly as much as not carrying out pre-scribed remedial exercises. Other reports have suggested that many athletes cannot even accurately describe the specific details of their recommended rehabilitation programme minutes after leaving the physiotherapy clinic! These are serious problems and in many cases will result in athletes returning to training or competition before the recovery process is complete.

> I've had about ten operations. I'm a bit like a battered old Escort. You might find one panel left that's original.
>
> *Ian Botham,*
> *former*
> *international*
> *cricketer*

Richard Cobbing, freestyle skier, who overcame a serious shoulder injury less than a year before he became the first British skier to win a world championship medal for over 50 years. Steve Bull helped Richard apply the principles of this chapter in the months leading up to his silver medal performance.

When athletes return to their sport too soon after an injury, they are frequently quite anxious and tense. They are worried about the injury and cannot relax and perform to their usual ability. Three significant problems subsequently arise:

1. Re-injury: Due to the tension arising from concern about the vulnerable area of the body, it is not uncommon for athletes to incur a different injury. By 'carrying' the primary injury, they have caused a new injury.

2.   Poor confidence: The tension and anxiety associated with the injury causes poor confidence and hence poor performance. A downward spiral of negative thinking and frustrating performance then results which can eventually lead to serious loss of self-esteem.

3.   Generally negative mood: Due to the interruption of the natural recovery process, psychological mood is low and this tends to drain the athlete's motivation and energy. In turn, performance suffers.

On account of these potential problems, athletes must be very wary of returning too soon after their injury and should always ensure that the rehabilitation has been successfully completed before contemplating a full return to training. Sometimes athletes need to resist pressure from coaches who attempt to exert inappropriate influence on the athlete's decision to return. Two typical examples of this exist. First, the coach who induces feelings of guilt in the athlete for letting the team down. And second, the coach who challenges the athlete's toughness by suggesting a harder athlete would play through the injury or be better able to tolerate the pain associated with performing again. Athletes must resist these attempts to short cut the recovery process and always consult a physiotherapist when in doubt about their readiness to return.

Social support

Sport psychologists around the world agree that one of the most significant factors in assisting athletes to stick with their rehabilitation programmes is the presence of social support. This support may be provided by a coach, a family member, a team-mate, a physiotherapist, a manager, a friend, etc.. It must be someone who is able to listen well, give sympathy when appropriate and assist in the process of adjustment and future optimism. Ideally, it will also be someone who is able to encourage the athlete to develop personal self-support. This involves establishing personal goals and objectives, agreeing with, and complying to, the rehabilitation programme, and being generally positive about the process of recovery. Research tells us that athletes who get this support process right tend to be the ones who recover well from injury and return to their sport with confidence and enthusiasm.

Nutritional advice

Part of the rehabilitation process may also involve consultation with a nutritionist. If an athlete's calorific expenditure has been dramatically reduced due to the inability to train vigorously, then some guidance on how to modify diet may be appropriate. This could be an important issue for athletes who are prone to put on weight and who are liable to become depressed when their body loses it's former composition.

Time with a physiotherapist

Athletes are more likely to stick with a rehabilitation programme if they meet the physiotherapist on a regular basis. During these meetings reinforcement can be given and the success of the rehabilitation can be adequately monitored.

Optimistic nature

If an athlete is a basically optimistic person, then a speedy, and successful recovery is more likely. Research in other areas of health care has shown that optimistic patients tend to make better recoveries.

Ability to plan ahead

Athletes must be capable of thinking, and planning, ahead. This is crucial for successful transition through the phases of reaction discussed earlier.

You might have bad luck like I had last year when I was laid up for six months and missed all my preparation for the season. But deep down inside me I knew that I could do well regardless.

Richard Cobbing, Silver Medalist at the 1993 Freestyle Aerials Skiing World Championships

Ability to deal with emotions

Injury recovery is an emotional period and athletes must be capable of dealing with the inevitable disappointment, anger, frustration, depression, etc..

Understanding of the process and involvement in decisions

Athletes need to understand the recovery and rehabilitation process. And, if they are involved in the associated decision-making, they are more likely to comply with physiotherapy instructions.

Mental training skills for the injured athlete

Canadian researchers Dr Lydia Ievleva and Dr Terry Orlick have shown that athletes who utilise mental training skills as a structured part of their injury rehabilitation programme recover quicker than athletes who do not. The three basic mental skills which these researchers identify are goal setting, positive self-talk and imagery. Each of these skills has been introduced earlier in this book but it is worth revisiting them in the context of how they may be used by an injured athlete.

Goal setting

It seems that the most useful form of goal setting for the injured athlete is daily goal setting. If small, but significant, daily goals are set, and achieved, by the injured athlete then it is likely that motivation and confidence will remain and the healing process will be enhanced. A daily goal setting process should therefore be carried out carefully, and usually in consultation with the physiotherapist. Effective daily goal setting will ensure that targets are specific, measurable, challenging and realistic. Some athletes like to set minimum goals as well as ideal goals. This is acceptable provided the minimum goals are challenging enough and the ideal goals are achievable. Again, the advice and experience of a physiotherapist is important here. Ten possible areas of focus in daily goal setting are:

1. flexibility gains;
2. strength gains;
3. speed gains;
4. endurance gains;
5. dietary aims;
6. imagery sessions;
7. relaxation sessions;
8. positive affirmation sessions;
9. technical gains;
10. rehabilitation programme achievements.

The tenth goal area in this list is particularly significant. As stated in the previous section, athletes simply MUST stick to their rehabilitation programmes and this includes periods of rest. Some athletes may even benefit from a form of behavioural contracting to assist this process whereby they actually sign an agreement with the physiotherapist to carry out the agreed regime of exercises.

Agreement is a key issue in the goal setting process. Athletes are unlikely to work hard towards goals if they have been 'imposed' upon them. Athletes need to feel part of the goal setting process (as discussed in chapter 2) and to feel a sense of ownership over the goals which are being stated. This will only be achieved if they have been consulted over the acceptability of the goals and the degree to which they feel that they can achieve them.

Longer term goal setting will also be helpful for most athletes. Having a structured vision of the future and knowing exactly what is being pursued is a powerful source of motivation and commitment. Athletes need to have a good idea of when they will be back to fitness so they can begin the process of mentally preparing for return to training and competition. Long term rehabilitation programmes get very boring and often disheartening. Having an end point towards which to work is vital if commitment is to be preserved.

So, a combination of daily and long term goals is one of the keys to facilitating a smooth rehabilitation programme. Communication with the physiotherapist, and usually the coach, is critical in getting this goal setting right but the athlete must be completely comfortable with the agreed targets and be fully committed to their achievement.

Positive self-talk

We have already identified an optimistic nature as being an important factor in the rehabilitation process. The use of positive self-talk is clearly associated with this. If injured athletes can think positively during their recovery it demonstrates an ability to accept the challenges ahead whilst working hard to achieve what is necessary to return to the desired level of performance. The research by Drs. Ievleva and Orlick demonstrated that athletes whose self-talk was positive, determined and encouraging recovered far quicker than those athletes who engaged in negative, whining and self-pitying self-talk.

Chapter 3 provides a detailed account of how athletes can improve their ability to use positive self-talk but specific

> Looking at it one way, I could say, 'I've been injured, I haven't been able to improve on my own British record, I haven't run well all season, and on top of all that my greatest rival keeps beating me!' Put like that it mounts up into a recipe for failure, a compendium of negative thoughts. It would amount to me psyching myself out, and would lead, inevitably, to defeat. However, when I focused on all this I could convert it into a positive version that not only made me feel much more optimistic, it gave me the motive to win. I said, in effect, 'the injury is slight, and my physiotherapist can deal with it. The record is mine, and no else's. I know how fast I am, I know how strong I am. I have never been better prepared than this. The season so far has been a build-up to the most important race, and I have not yet peaked. And Sandra (Farmer-Patrick) is going into the Olympics as the favourite in our event; no one expects me to be able to beat her, and so all the pressure will be on her, not on me.'
>
> *Sally Gunnell*, *Olympic Gold Medalist and World Champion hurdler*

examples of positive, and negative, thinking relating to injury are shown below.

Examples of positive and negative self-talk relating to sports injury

Positive self-talk:

"How can I make the most out of what I can do now?"
"I can beat this thing."
"I can do anything."
"I told myself, 'I can do it'. I can beat the odds and recover sooner than normal."
"I want to go spring skiing. I'll be totally healed by then."
"I have to work to get my leg as strong as the other one."
"It's feeling pretty good."
"It's getting better all the time."

Negative self-talk:

"It's probably going to take forever to get better."
"I'll never make up for the lost time."
"What a stupid thing to do — dumb mistake."
"What a useless body."
"It will never be as strong again."
"Stupid fool! Stupid injury. Stupid leg."
"I talked to myself about how frustrated I was. There is nothing good about this and there is nothing I can do about it."
"Why me?"

[Taken from Ievleva & Orlick (1993). 'Mental paths to enhanced recovery'. In *Psychological Bases of Sport Injury*. Edited by D. Pargman. Copyright © from Fitness Information Technology, Inc. Morgantown, WV 26504, USA (304-599-3482). Reprinted with permission.]

So, injured athletes should monitor their internal dialogue and attempt to maintain a positive focus as much as possible. When they find themselves slipping into negative mode, they should immediately focus on something positive in their rehabilitation programme — this, of course, is where the daily goals will be extremely useful.

Imagery

The value of using imagery to assist healing processes dates back to ancient Eastern philosophies. Athletes can use imagery during injury recovery in two basic ways. First, it can be used to actually facilitate the healing of the injury. In this case, the athlete visualises the injured body part getting stronger and returning to normal functioning. Second, it can be used to promote performance confidence. In this case, the athlete visualises returning to training and competition successfully.

The list below provides specific examples of the type of images athletes can engage in within these two basic areas.

Summary of imagery application during rehabilitation

1. *Visualising the healing taking place to the injured area internally.*

2. *Visualising effectively moving through specific motions and situations that put the most demand on the injured area.*

3. *Re-experiencing or imagining individual skills required for best performance — to stay sharp mentally.*

4. *Calling up the feelings that characterise best performance.*

5. *Visualising returning to competition and performing at one's best.*

6. *Engaging in imagery that involves feeling positive, enthusiastic, and confident about returning to training and competition.*

We recommend that injured athletes set aside regular periods for imagery practice. The more inactive they are, the more imagery they can do. We suggest a combination of healing and performance imagery with the emphasis shifting as return to training approaches. In the early days of recovery, more time should be spent on healing imagery. As recovery progresses, the focus can become more performance-related.

Concluding note

We hope you never get injured! But the chances are, that if you're a serious athlete, you probably will. However, if you have prepared a positive recovery plan, the potential impact of this injury will be greatly reduced and you'll be able to bounce back strong and confident.

A suitable anecdote with which to finish this chapter is provided by Professor Bruce Tuckman from Florida State University. As a very keen recreational marathon runner he described his own experiences of a serious back injury in the book *Psychological Bases of Sport Injuries* [full reference is given at the foot of p. 136]. In his description he recounts the adage "I cried because I had no shoes.....and then I met a man with no feet." Professor Tuckman explains that no matter how badly off we feel we are, there is always someone whose situation is worse. He suggests that remembering this may help athletes in putting their personal calamities in perspective.

The injury recovery funda*MENTAL*s

1. *Accept the injury and be aware of its nature and severity.*

2. *Set daily goals which provide a pathway to achieving the long term goal of return to training and competition.*

3. *Emphasise the positive aspects in the recovery process.*

4. *Practise positive self-talk on a daily basis and use it especially when negative thoughts arise.*

5. *Use imagery as a way of feeling the injured body part recover.*

6. *Use imagery to prepare for a confident, and successful, return to training and competition.*

Chapter 8
Group dynamics: The team plan

The self-belief of the players, engendered by Dermott Reeve but infectious to all, is a wonder of the modern county game, for Warwickshire do not boast a collection of outstanding individuals but, far more unusually, a truly outstanding team.

Alan Lee,
cricket correspondent for *The Times Newspaper*, 1995

If you are a member of a team, or a group of athletes who train together, then there are certain sport psychology principles which are worth considering. Your role on the team is important to a number of other athletes as well as yourself. In order for the team, or group, to demonstrate high team spirit, all individuals must be comfortable in their role and be totally committed to the team effort. When this happens, it is possible that a group of players can produce a team performance which exceeds the sum of each individual's ability. This is sometimes referred to as 'synergy' and an example is referred to in the above quote about Warwickshire cricket team.

So, our opening recommendation in this chapter, is to focus on your job as a team member. Do everything you can to ensure that you will do your job to the best of your ability. Avoid worrying about other members of the team or group.

Don't be distracted by the demands of other positions — concentrate on the successful execution of your skills. In order to facilitate this process, an examination of the psychology of individual roles is worthwhile.

Individual roles in sports groups

In his book *Group Dynamics in Sport*, Dr Albert Carron (an internationally renowned expert in the area) outlines the importance of role behaviours in the effectiveness of a sports team. He explains that as a team develops, strategical plans are established and individual members of the team are assigned certain roles within those plans. Team members are allocated formal roles pertaining to performance on the field, as well as informal roles such as team clown, social secretary or minibus driver. Three conditions must exist in order for there to be a link between individual roles and team effectiveness. These are illustrated in the figure below.

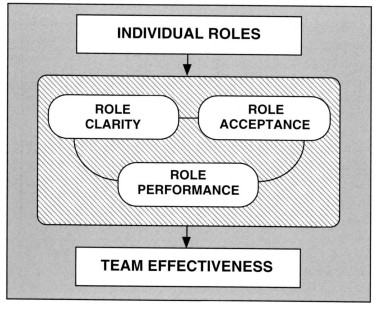

Taken from *Group Dynamics in Sport*,
A. V. Carron, 1988, Sports Dynamics

Role clarity

This refers to the extent to which players are clear about their role on the team or in the group. It is not uncommon for athletes to be confused about their role and consequently feel unsure about how they should approach performance. This lack of clarity usually leads to a lack of confidence and sometimes to arguments and conflict between different members within the group. An example of lack of role clarity was illustrated by some members of the England Women's Cricket Team who were involved in a discussion prior to the European Cup in 1990. One player expressed her confusion and lack of confidence about her supposed role on the team. Four other players involved in the small group were surprised at her feelings, and proceeded to explain the value of her contribution to the team and how they specifically perceived her role. It transpired that the player's role was different from that when she played for her club side, but she was encouraged and motivated by her teammates' open support and

> The atmosphere and the ethos that was built up with the sport psychology got us into that frame of mind, being positive and encouraging, and it just became automatic really.
>
> *Barbara Daniels, Member of the 1993 World Cup winning England Women's Cricket Team*

> My advice to anyone competing at the Olympics is simple — don't get caught up in the emotions. That's the thing that will sap you. Try to stay unaware of how your teammates are going. You can't help them and they can't help you. Ignore the hype and concentrate on your performance.
>
> *Carl Lewis, Olympic sprint and long jump champion*

clarification. Afterwards she said:

> "I have become a lot more confident as a team member. I have found it difficult to understand and establish the role I play, but after this discussion I feel a lot more accepted by the squad."

Role acceptance

This refers to the extent to which players are satisfied with the role which has been allocated to them. Players may demonstrate a high degree of role clarity — i.e., they are fully aware of what is expected of them — but not be happy with the role. Lack of role acceptance can have serious effects on team spirit although with discussion and negotiation, problems can often be resolved.

> I study their games to see what they can do and what they can't. I try and help them with what they're not good at, tell them my weaknesses and hopefully we learn from each other. The sooner the partnership clicks the better you're both going to play.
>
> *Teddy Sheringham, international soccer player discussing forging a good partnership with another striker*

Perceived role performance

This refers to the extent to which players are perceived to be actually carrying out their roles with success. If role clarity and role acceptance are present, but perceived role performance is not occurring, then team cohesion will be affected. An important perspective on perceived role performance within teams or other sports groups, is the issue of appreciating the roles of teammates. It is not uncommon for athletes to be unaware of the specific demands of other positions in the team and hence be quick to criticise when mistakes are made. Teams which have a full appreciation of the various

One player may score, but every member of the team must perform a role successfully along the way.

demands of different positions invariably demonstrate higher levels of cohesion and work better together when under stress. We feel it's very important that athletes get some experience of the demands of performing in another position and fulfilling another role. This is best achieved by spending time talking with teammates about the demands of their position. Even playing in that position during training time occasionally (provided this does not present a potential chance of injury) has proved to be an enlightening experience for some athletes. Typically, after doing this, athletes report that they are less likely to criticise teammates during a competition because they have an appreciation of the nature of the challenges of performing in that position.

So, if the three conditions of role clarity, role acceptance and perceived role performance are met, then team cohesion will be enhanced and it is likely that team performance will improve. Also, individuals within the team or group, will feel happier and more committed to their training and performance preparation.

Dealing with substitution

Most athletes in team sports have to deal with being dropped or substituted at some time in their careers. For many, this can be an extremely damaging blow to confidence and can also lead to de-motivation and other attitude problems. So, dealing with substitution is an important skill to acquire, even though you may only have to use it very infrequently. The term benchwarmer has emerged in recent years for an athlete who has been dropped, removed from the starting line-up, or substituted. Studies have shown that benchwarmers typically exhibit a range of emotional reactions to their situation which, in turn, present special challenges which need to be overcome if confidence and motivation are to remain high. A number of these challenges are listed below.

Dr Deidre Connelly, from the College of William and Mary in Virginia, identifies five basic strategies for athletes who find themselves in this situation and who may be experiencing any of the emotional reactions identified in the list opposite. The following explanation of these strategies has also been adapted, with permission, from *Performance Edge, The Letter of Performance Psychology* (Nov/Dec, 1992, pp.5-6).

Recognise the additional work and commitment required of a non-starter

Non-starters often must work that bit harder to remain confident and highly motivated. A high level of commitment to sport is needed to get through times when you're not selected. It's useful to acknowledge, and remember, that as you progress up the sporting ladder, the chances for success decrease — in other words, the competition increases.

Develop your self-confidence

Self-confidence is crucial to successful performance as we have described earlier in the book. Utilising appropriate positive self-talk relating to your place in a team is therefore

Special challenges for the benchwarmer

- *Not feeling part of the win.*

- *Feeling like you could have done better than others who got to play and "lost" the game.*

- *Never getting to play with the starters and, therefore, feeling like you'll never improve.*

- *Being asked to time, score, videotape or bring water during breaks in play.*

- *Being put into the game with only a few minutes left on the clock.*

- *Riding home on the bus listening to your teammates discuss the game and how they played, and having nothing to say.*

- *Never getting your kit dirty.*

- *Having to answer the question, "Did you play?".*

- *Playing with the 2nd team because you were dropped from the Firsts.*

- *Feeling bitter, rejected, isolated or incompetent.*

Adapted from Connelly (1992). The Benchwarmer.
Performance Edge, The Letter of Performance Psychology , Nov/Dec, p. 2.
PO Box 842, Carrboro, NC (USA) 27510-0842. Reproduced with permission.

important. To facilitate this, you must learn to identify your strengths and weaknesses within your team and then decide what you must do to feel good about your specific contribution.

Recognise the factors which you can, and can't, control

Accept the things over which you have no control. Stop "fighting" issues which cannot be resolved in your favour and don't waste energy and effort feeling unnecessarily sorry for yourself or angry. Accept coaches' decisions and avoid taking things personally. Remind yourself why you are playing this sport — because you enjoy it!

Keep lines of communication open with your coaches

This may be difficult because you are disappointed over not playing, or frustrated at not being given a chance. Nevertheless, some sort of feedback will be helpful, provided you can take it as constructive advice. Remind yourself that you're a valued member of this team in ways other than always being in the starting line-up.

Be ready to play at any time

You must maintain a positive image at all times and give the impression that you are ready to perform at any time. Spend time with positive people who support you. Resist the temptation to hang around with others who are not playing and complaining about selection issues. If you do get a chance to play, don't try heroic acts when the spotlight is on you. Make sure you get the basics right and do your job well. Trying too hard may lead to anxiety and errors. Think in the present and be sure to reward yourself when you do something well.

Team motivation

As with individual performance, motivation is a vital element of team functioning. If the team is not motivated as a group, as well as at the individual level, performance will suffer. Several factors are of notable attention to ensure that team motivation is at its highest.

Team goal setting

Many sports teams do not meet formally at the beginning of a season to identify their competitive and training goals for the forthcoming season. We feel this is a mistake. The absence of agreed, and formalised team goals, often leads to a range of problems such as reduced commitment, lack of adherence to training standards, conflict between team members and a general lack of direction during both preparation and competition. So, encourage your team to have a goal setting plan. Suggest formal meetings are set up to facilitate the goal setting process. When these meetings have been set up, utilise an adaptation of the profiling process to assist in the process of establishing a team game plan.

Team Profiling

We outlined the Performance Profiling technique in chapter 2. This process can be used with your team to provide a base for setting season's goals. The process lets the team develop its own goals, and you can use these to supplement any goal programme that has already been set for the team. Review the fundamentals of the profiling process and make the following adjustments.

1   Get the team to identify an ideal team, or a picture of the team at the peak of its potential.

2   Have the team identify all the qualities that make up this ideal or peak team. Do this by getting the team to carry out a brainstorming exercise for five or ten minutes to list as many qualities as possible. Use of a flip chart will assist this process. Then have the team review all the qualities to make sure that there is a consensus agreement on each factor's inclusion.

3   Have the team produce a target, "ideal" value for each of the qualities.

4   Get the team to produce a consensus current score for each of the qualities.

5   Work out the discrepancy between the ideal and current scores.

6   Select the qualities with the largest discrepancy scores. You can now go about designing specific training and competition strategies to help improve these performance areas.

As well as carrying out this process with the whole team, you may find that you can use the same approach to encourage communication and self-evaluation in sub-units of the team such as defensive and offensive units.

Open communication channels

Teams need to have open communication channels whereby players can discuss issues amongst themselves and sometimes provide feedback, and suggestions, for the coaching staff.

Problems must be discussed rather than bottled up. Issues need to be confronted and solutions considered in a democratic way.

Of course, the time for open discussion is not in the period immediately preceding competition. This is where strong, and confident, leadership is required. However, in the more relaxed atmosphere of training sessions, there should be plenty of opportunities for reflection and discussion.

Understanding individual differences

Athlete vary immensely in personality. One of the reasons why Mike Brearley is always remembered as being an extremely good captain of the England Cricket Team was that he was able to appreciate these differences and interact with players accordingly. He knew that some players required a strong, authoritarian approach and would respond to being treated accordingly. Other players, however, required a more 'softly-softly' approach. These players needed lots of

> **Cooke possessed a well-organised and analytical mind.... He quickly introduced the idea of joint responsibility..... Here, at last, was the opportunity to give voice to our thoughts and to express our views without fear of retribution. In the bad old days the sharp and, very often, not so short shock for players who had lost form was to drop them, but here was someone advocating player participation.**
>
> *Rob Andrew, discussing Geoff Cooke and his management style of the England Rugby Team*

encouragement and social support in times of crisis, when the pressure was on. By treating players differently in this way, Brearley was able to "get the most out of his team". In a sense, Brearley was being a psychologist, as well as captain.

We believe that all members of a team should have an appreciation of the different personalities of their teammates. This is achieved, again, by open discussion and by the sharing of personal preferences and attitudes.

One practical example of this, which we have used successfully in our practice, is to encourage each member of a team to explain to the rest of the team, how they wish to be treated when they are under-performing or have made a mistake. Some athletes prefer to be left alone in this situation. Others acknowledge that they would respond to a "kick in the pants!". It's important that each member of the team is aware of these preferences in order to avoid inappropriate, albeit well-meaning, attempts to help a teammate through such a crisis.

> **When the (England) B squad met before matches he (Alan Davies) would pre-arrange the dinner table settings so that players from different clubs sat together. He would make certain that forwards and backs were mixed together and would then issue each table with a questionnaire about the forthcoming game. That way he encouraged immediate communication between the different groups and personalities, some of whom might not otherwise have addressed a word to each other from the moment the team assembled until, three days later, when they disappeared. Davies hated cliques.**
>
> *Rob Andrew,*
> *discussing the*
> *management style of*
> *Alan Davies*

"90 per cent of players are uplifted and perform better by being told they are good players. Only 10 per cent need constantly kicking up the backside."

Gary Lineker, former soccer international

Another example relates to the pre-competition period. Some coaches, or captains, have a pre-match style which involves talking a lot with players. This approach invariably involves plenty of back slapping and encouragement. However, some athletes do not appreciate this and prefer to be left alone. They know how best to prepare and the intrusion of others, even if it is the coach, is dis–ruptive. Consequently, a well-intentioned supportive chat from the coach may actually prevent the athlete from getting into the ideal performance state.

Commitment to positive thinking

Teams need to make a commitment to positive thinking in the same way that individual athletes must. Mutual encouragement and support through thick and thin is vital if team cohesion is to remain high. Teammates can help contribute to this by reminding each other to

When the pressure really hit us, we became stronger as a team. Yes, we had arguments, but we all wanted to achieve the same thing — success. We simply had to remind ourselves that this was basically just another hockey tournament where the world's best teams were playing. Nothing else, nothing complicated — just hockey matches.

Robert Clift, *Hockey Olympic Gold Medalist*

Every time Stocky and I met in the middle we told each other we could do it and eventually we really believed it. In the end it was thoroughly enjoyable. I went through one phase of doubt but just kept saying positive things.

Clare Taylor, *England cricketer, after batting with Debbie Stock for a 90 minute last wicket stand to draw the final Test match and win the 1995 series in India*

use positive self-talk and to stay focused during pressure periods.

A favourite technique used by sport psychologists to foster this positive thinking at the individual level is to run an exercise in which each member of the team writes something positive about each teammate. This can be done either anonymously or with signatures. All comments are then collated and an individual list is compiled for each team member containing all the positive comments relating to them. Sometimes these individual lists are distributed immediately although it is sometimes appropriate to keep the lists and hand them out at a specific time such as the evening before an important match. Although perhaps not necessary for all athletes, techniques like this have been found to be extremely effective for athletes who have a tendency to doubt their ability or their worthiness on a team. It can be very reassuring to read a list of positive comments made by people who will be performing alongside you. Of additional value, is the significant effect this type of positive thinking exercise can have on team spirit.

Team spirit

One of the outstanding things about being in the squad was the team spirit; it was excellent. The sport psychology input can only have helped that.

Barbara Daniels,
England cricketer,
after the team had
won the 1993
World Cup

There are many things an individual athlete can do within a team setting to promote mutual confidence and team spirit. Before describing some of these strategies, it is important to clarify the exact nature of team spirit. In the sport psychology literature, team spirit is referred to as team (or group) cohesion. It has been demonstrated that there are two different types of cohesion — social and task. **Social cohesion** refers to the extent to which players get on with each other on a social basis.

Recommendations for team building

Team Identity

Get athletes together in advance of competition.

Set up residential training camps if possible.

Provide the team with unique identifiers such as blazers, ties, logos, kit and mottos.

Emphasise any unique history or traditions within the team.

Recognise the importance of pride in the team and develop its sources.

Team structure

Develop a team structure in which there is a clear differentiation in team roles.

Clarify role expectations for members and allow time for group discussions relating to role differentiation.

Establish consensus and agreement on status differences within the team.

Team goals

Ensure that the team sets clear and realistic goals.

Clarify how adherence to team standards facilitates team effectiveness.

Ensure the team is provided with appropriate feedback on the achievement of goals.

Promote cooperation and discourage individual rivalry.

Team motivation

Help individuals identify personal needs and goals and clarify how these can be satisfied in a team context.

Encourage significant team members to make sacrifices for the team.

Instil in each team member a sense of responsibility for the team's success.

High levels of social cohesion are exhibited by teams which spend time together off the field and enjoy each other's company in non-sport related situations. **Task cohesion** refers to the extent to which team members agree on the goals of the team and the strategies which are employed to achieve those goals. It is therefore possible for a team to be high on one aspect of cohesion and low in the other. Nevertheless, most teams attempt to attain high levels of social AND task cohesion as it is assumed that performance is increased when team members are socially integrated as well as being united in their efforts on the field of play.

According to Dr Albert Carron, in his book "Group Dynamics in Sport", team building strategies can relate to four different aspects of team functioning — team identity, team structure, team goals and team motives. A summary of a number of recommendations for team building based on these four aspects is presented on p. 153. We suggest that you review this list and then consider which strategies may be particularly useful for your sport — and specifically, your team.

The team dynamics funda*MENTAL*s

1. *Ensure that all individuals on a team contribute to the achievement of role clarity, role acceptance and perceived role performance.*

2. *Create a supportive network for athletes who are benched and encourage these athletes to maintain a positive and committed outlook.*

3. *Set team goals by using a profiling procedure and create an atmosphere of open communication (at appropriate times) and dialogue.*

4. *Appreciate the contrast in personalities within a team and ensure all members are sensitive to these differences.*

5. *Encourage positive thinking at the individual, and team, levels.*

6. *Utilise appropriate team building strategies relating to the identity, structure, goals and motivation of the group.*

Chapter 9
Competition preparation: The professional plan

You need discipline in your lifestyle, because that affects anybody's achievement factor. Show me somebody who's not 'tight' in the disciplines of living, and I'll show you somebody who hasn't reached the limit of their true potential. People have a way of getting sloppy and when you get sloppy you get careless. You forget things, there's not the same attention to detail.

Jackie Stewart,
former World Champion Motor Racing Driver

Having a 'professional' attitude or 'being professional' towards sport does not only refer to those who are paid to participate. Being professional refers to choices you make and the responsibilities you accept. Any individual who is serious about performing consistently and achieving sporting potential should have a 'professional' attitude. The ultimate in being professional is a way of behaving so that everything you do supports your ability to perform. Being professional is managing, in an advantageous way, those things that you can control, not trying to manage those things you cannot control,

> **Everyone has a will to win, but very few have a will to prepare.**
>
> *Vince Lombardi, American football coach after whom the Superbowl trophy is named*

and being able to tell the difference.

Being professional is a way of life. It is a way of thinking about one's self, about one's sport, about other people and a way of doing things with pride. In short, it is a way of behaving. Becoming professional in sport involves bringing more and more aspects of one's life into harmony with the goals and aspirations one has in sport. Being professional is wanting to perform your best at all times and committing yourself to doing everything possible to make that happen.

Adopting a professional attitude

In order to achieve their potential in sport, athletes must be 'professional' in the way they approach training, competition, social life, work/school life, family life, nutrition, and the prevention of injury. It is professional to order things in such a way that all aspects of life permit the athlete to enter competition in a state of body and mind that will allow the maximum performance possible. To achieve this, athletes must take charge of their preparation and create situations which will make things happen — rather than expecting everything to fit nicely into place and waiting for things to happen. The professional athlete accepts the responsibility to make choices which will support optimal performance while unprofessional athletes let others determine outcomes.

Being professional in sport, involves a number of complementary areas (see examples listed opposite). It relates to the choices you make about how you spend your time, how you treat other people, how you eat, how you sleep, how you control your mind, how you react to things that you can control and to those things you cannot control. It is about

Examples of the professional approach in sport

- *Having a nutritionally balanced diet which allows the body to work hard in practice, to recover properly, and to perform in competition.*

- *Arriving at practices on time in a frame of mind that is not distracted by earlier events in the day and ready to expend maximum effort.*

- *Occupying time the night before a competition preparing physically and mentally — reviewing opponents and competition strategies, checking equipment, and getting the required amount of sleep.*

- *Behaving towards teammates or training partners in a way that expresses confidence in their abilities and in a way that allows them to prepare themselves for competition.*

- *Taking responsibility for mistakes and working hard to correct them.*

accepting responsibility for how you prepare and how you react. It is about planning for choices which will permit you to perform to your ability. In short, it is professional to have a healthy obsession for ordering your life and preparation for competition.

This type of planning is an important aspect of being professional. All individuals who approach a task professionally do so with a plan. Planning is more than making a list of things TO DO or ordering such a list by immediate priority of urgency or importance. Professional planning and preparation takes place over a much longer period of time. Depending on the level at which you compete it may be anything between one week and four years.

Laura Davies, whose professional competition preparation has resulted in numerous tournament wins.

> **The intelligent approach to golf includes planning your round. If it's important enough to you, spend time visualising how you are going to play each hole... When I'm at a tournament, I stay in my hotel room after dinner. I call home to talk to my wife and kids; then I think about how I'm going to play the next round. I go over it hole by hole, like a pitcher going over the hitters he will face in the next game. I keep notebooks in which I analyse shots I hit in earlier rounds or previous tournaments and I study it... I'll assure you that the more time you spend planning and visualising, the better you'll play.**
>
> *Ray Floyd, former champion golfer*

The training review

To encourage athletes to take control of their competition preparation with a profess-ional attitude, we have used a **Training Review Chart** (see following page) as a technique for monitoring ongoing com-mitment and determination to achieve goals. The chart pre-sents a series of ten questions relating to different aspects of performance preparation. Athletes are asked to rate their satisfaction with their own preparation on a scale of one to ten. The sum of the ten dif-ferent ratings provides an overall rating for the chosen assessment period with a maximum score of 100. Typi-cally, a chart would be com-pleted every two weeks, but this may vary according to the athlete, the sport or the time of the season.

If the ratings are favour-able, then the chart should be a useful source of confidence, pride and positive feeling. The athlete is preparing in a pro-fessional manner and is doing as much as possible to ensure progress and improvement. If, however, the ratings are not so good, the chart highlights the areas where preparation is not

TRAINING REVIEW CHART

NAME: DATE:

Training and Preparation

I would give myself the following ratings for the previous phase:

	LOW.........AVERAGE.........HIGH
Staying positive even when performing badly	1 2 3 4 5 6 7 8 9 10
Giving 100% in technical training	1 2 3 4 5 6 7 8 9 10
Giving 100% in fitness training	1 2 3 4 5 6 7 8 9 10
Doing regular "high quality" imagery training	1 2 3 4 5 6 7 8 9 10
Eating enough of the right foods	1 2 3 4 5 6 7 8 9 10
Monitoring my fluid intake	1 2 3 4 5 6 7 8 9 10
Ensuring equipment is in best possible condition	1 2 3 4 5 6 7 8 9 10
Taking personal responsibility for mistakes and working hard to correct them	1 2 3 4 5 6 7 8 9 10
Focusing on the controllables	1 2 3 4 5 6 7 8 9 10
Dealing with the daily hassles that bother me	1 2 3 4 5 6 7 8 9 10
OVERALL TRAINING RATING OUT OF 100	

Training and Preparation goals for next phase:

1.
2.
3.
4.

as professional as it could be and where commitment may be lacking. The scoring procedure should serve to initiate a change in attitude over the forthcoming assessment period. It may also influence training goals which are listed for the forthcoming phase at the bottom of the chart.

We would encourage you to develop your own personal training review chart which is specific to the requirements of your sport. After you've created your own chart, use it for a trial period of two or three months and then perhaps it will need refining.

Preparation routines

Another strategy we have used a great deal in our work is the use of competition preparation routines. In chapter 5 we discussed the implementation of immediate pre-performance routines as a technique for controlling attention. We'll now expand this idea and discuss how athletes can develop routines which will help guide professional behaviour before, during and after competitions. We divide the time periods around competition into different blocks (shown below) and suggest that athletes should develop specific routines for each of these blocks.

Time periods requiring planned routines

1. *Long term pre-competition*
2. *Short term pre-competition*
3. *Night before competition*
4. *Competition morning wake-up to departure for venue*
5. *Arrival at competition venue*
6. *Pre-competition warm-up*
7. *Competition*
8. *Post-competition*

Different sports will vary in the importance of these time periods. One specific time period may be far more important in one sport than in another due to the demands of the situation. Nevertheless, we recommend that athletes consider each time period and develop some sort of structured routine so that nothing is left to chance. So, before we go any further, we recommend that you acquire a note book which is allocated as your competition routine log. You'll need lots of blank pages to allow you to experiment with different routines for each of the eight identified time periods.

> **Thorough preparation is the best way to avoid the unexpected. There are several related factors that work together to build mental security. Basically, it comes down to two questions. Have I done everything possible to prepare myself? Have I prepared correctly and with 100% effort? These questions must be asked constantly.**
>
> *Mac Wilkins, USA Olympic field athlete*

Why are routines important?

One of the key purposes of developing, and implementing, competition routines is to establish a consistent approach to performance. In order for consistency to occur, a plan must exist for eliminating controllable distracters such as forgetting a key piece of equipment — a mistake which has happened many times to world class athletes! And, a plan must exist for focusing attention on controllable performance enhancers such as arousal management as discussed in chapter 6. Routines facilitate both of these aspects of preparation. They provide the athlete with a detailed protocol to follow so that attentional focus, confidence and anxiety control are all working together to maximise the chances of attaining the ideal performance state. A familiar set of competition routines will

> **Winning can be defined as the science of being totally prepared.**
>
> *George Allen, US sportswriter*

give the athlete a framework whereby attention is constantly focused on the things that are important and this concentration is not disturbed by uncontrollable, and irrelevant, distractions.

So, let's work through each of the eight time periods and identify the range of elements which need to be considered at each of these stages. Clearly, all elements identified will not be relevant to all sports. You need to decide which are the critical elements for your sport, omit the others, and then begin to devise your own personal routine incorporating the elements which you have identified as being important.

1   Long term pre-competition

This period ends the week before competition commences and can begin at any period in advance of this time. This routine is particularly important for competitions which require international travel, are known well in advance, or are highly significant performances. The following items need to be considered:

1. Travel documents updated — passport, immunisation records, insurance.

2. Sport documents in order — governing body accreditation details.

3. Arrangements made with school, university or employer regarding time away.

4. Plan for adjusting to climate change.

5. Plan for dealing with jet lag.

6. Plan for acquiring information about competition site, accommodation and availability of food.

7. Plan for post-competition travel if not with team.

8. Plan for occupying travel time and dealing with boredom.

The day of the competition I try to run my routine identical to what I usually do.

Bob Molle, 1984 Olympic Wrestling Silver Medalist

...I went back to the (Olympic) village. Already I was timing how long the bus journey took. A significant part of my preparation for an event is to make myself familiar with the practical details, so that when the time comes I can't be suddenly thrown off course by, say, missing a bus or not knowing where the toilet is.

Sally Gunnell, Olympic Gold Medalist and World Champion hurdler

Going to Cardiff two days before the match, rather than on the Saturday morning as had been our custom, was part of Cooke's psychological build-up for the opening Championship game against Wales. Our preparations had begun on the Wednesday evening at Kingsholm in Gloucester where the manager had organised a special St. David's Day welcome for us. As we ran on to the field the tannoy crackled into life with a scratchy rendition of the Welsh national anthem. As we crossed the Severn Bridge the following day, the anthem was played again on the team bus, and for the next forty-eight hours, we were immersed in all things Welsh. By the time we walked through the packed lobby of our hotel an hour and half before kickoff and began our solemn march to the ground through thousands of milling supporters, we were totally immune to the Welsh and Wales.

Rob Andrew, discussing preparation for victory at Cardiff Arms Park

2   Short term pre-competition

This period begins a week before the competition starts and ends on the evening before. The following items need to be considered:

1.   Acquire information about the competition site.
2.   Acquire information about the opposition.
3.   Check on availability of food and drink facilities.
4.   Check on the details of travel and accommodation.
5.   Check and pack competition equipment.
6.   Check and pack other relevant personal belongings.
7.   Purchase and pack any special food or drinks for the competition site.
8.   Review competition day routines.

3   Night before competition

This period may require two different routines — one for home events and one for away events. The distracters and enhancers may be different in these two situations. However, the more similar they are, the better. The following items need to be considered:

1.   Timing of team meeting or meeting with coach.
2.   Eating arrangements.
3.   Final equipment check.
4.   Relaxation activities.
5.   Review of competition strategy.
6.   Mental rehearsal of performance.
7.   Positive self-talk.
8.   Appropriate sleep.

> **At last the morning came, and because the heats were early in the day's events I had to be up early. I set the alarm for 5.00am, but I had been practising even that for the last two days so it didn't come as a great shock to the system.**
>
> **Sally Gunnell**, *discussing race preparation in the 1992 Olympics*

4   Wake up to departure time

This period may vary from an hour to many hours and therefore must be adjusted accordingly. The following items need to be considered:

1.   Wake up routine — first thoughts and feelings.
2.   Washing/showering procedures.
3.   Eating time.
4.   Final final equipment check!
5.   Team meeting or meeting with coach.
6.   Relaxation activities.
7.   Jogging or stretching routines.
8.   Positive self-talk.

5   Arrival at competition venue

Again, the available time in this period may vary greatly so any routine must be capable of being adjusted accordingly. The following items need to be considered:

1.   Familiarise with competition site — toilets, locker rooms, food arrangements.
2.   Inspect the competition site — mental rehearsal of successful performance.
3.   Positive self-talk.
4.   Locate personal space and "settle in".

6   Pre-competition warm-up

This routine should be extremely consistent and very well-rehearsed. It should have been practised in training numerous times. The following items need to be considered:

1.   Physical elements — jogging, stretching and technical rehearsal.
2.   Final review of opposition strengths and weaknesses.
3.   Final review of competition strategy.
4.   Final mental rehearsal.
5.   Final positive self-talk.
6.   Use of key words or phrases.
7.   Arousal check — followed by arousal management strategies if necessary.

7   Competition

Again, any competition routines must be very consistent and have been practised over and over in training. The chapter on attentional control covers the type of routines an athlete should use during the actual competition phase. The following items need to be considered:

1.   Pre-performance routines.
2.   Routines for dealing with errors.
3.   Routines for dealing with distractions.
4.   Appropriate use of self-talk.
5.   Appropriate use of concentration cues.
6.   Appropriate use of mental imagery.

8   Post-competition

The post-competition period is often overlooked by athletes who feel that once the competition has finished there is nothing else that can be done. This is a mistake. Much can be achieved in the post-competition period and the establishment of an appropriate routine will maximise the chances of superior performance occurring in the next competition. We feel that the best approach to developing a suitable post-competition routine is to use a *"recycling system"*. We use a system consisting of six elements. To aid memory, each elements begins with the letter 'R':

1   *React*:   It is acceptable to have an emotional reaction following competition. This reaction may be a satisfied and enjoyable one or it may be one of frustration and disappointment. The important thing is that the reaction allows athletes to release pent-up emotions and get feelings out of their system. This is healthy as long as the reactions do not interfere with future training and competition preparation.

2   *Relax*:   This relaxation should include both physical and mental aspects. It is a process of warming down and cooling off. It will vary immensely between different sports and different individuals.

3   *Refresh*:   This represents a routine of showering, taking in food and liquids, and dealing with any physical ailments that may need attention.

4   *Review*:   A performance review process has been discussed earlier in the book in the confidence chapter where we described the good and bad points list technique. Something of this nature is an important part of the post-competition routine process. The process may also include recording notes on the opposition which are kept for future reference and used as part of the pre-competition routine for another performance.

5   *Refocus*:   After the performance review it's important to leave the past behind and look ahead positively to the future. A diversion of attention away from your sport is sometimes an effective way of achieving this. Following this diversion, it is then possible, and important, to refocus attention on the next set of training and performance goals.

6   *Re-enter*:   It is now time to re-enter the preparation process — perhaps at the long-term, or short-term

preparation stage. The state of this re-entry will clearly depend on the sport and the typical length of time between competitive experiences. A marathon runner competing once or twice a year will clearly be on a different time frame from a tennis player competing several times per week.

A final note on this recycling routine concerns athletes taking part in tournament sports where they may be competing more than once in a day. For these athletes, it's important to establish a workable recycling routine which contains each of the six elements but which can be carried out after each performance.

Developing your own competition routines

Now that we have introduced you to each of the different time periods requiring a routine, you are ready to develop your own personalised versions. We cannot prescribe the best routines for you and your sport because there is so much room for variability and personal preference. You probably need to discuss your preparation with a coach and/or with teammates.

It's also useful to observe very successful performers in your sport to identify how they approach competition preparation. Then you can begin to develop your own special routines. You may wish to combine, in a way that is appropriate for the demands of your sport, some of the 8 time periods we have discussed.

An example of this combined approach is provided in the sample pre-competition plan (see following page) which describes a pre-competition routine from the night before competition through to the commencement of performance and uses a countdown approach. We have adapted this routine from one described by our colleague Brian Miller, who worked for several years preparing athletes at the Australian Institute of Sport.

Sample pre-competition plan

10 The night before:

Prepare equipment bag and check contents thoroughly. Shower and relax (listen to music, read). Spend 20 minutes relaxing and listening to calming music. Conduct an imagery session in which you see yourself performing really well tomorrow.

9 About 7.00am:

Wake up and go for an early morning jog. While on the run, start to image the competition and run through your tactics. Shower and breakfast.

8 Between 9.00 and 10.30am:

Go through the competition plan and consider how you will respond if certain events disrupt your ideal preparation. Decide how you will deal with any inconveniences.

7 10.30am:

Go to the competition venue. Go to the marshalling area and report in.

6 11.30am:

Check your equipment. Have a light snack.

5 Approximately 1.00pm:

Go to the warm-up area and begin some gentle jogging. Soak up the atmosphere and conditions so that you know what to expect immediately prior to performance.

4 Approximately 2.00pm:

Check your arousal level. There's 30 minutes until the start. How are you feeling? Do you need to pump up or calm down? Are you in The Zone?

3 Approximately 2.10pm:

Final check of your equipment. Spend 2-3 minutes imaging the start of competition. Begin the final phase of your warm-up routine.

2 Approximately 2.20pm:

Repeat some positive self-statements which you have worked on in practice. Remind yourself of some of your previous good performances.

1 2.27pm:

Final check of pre-competition arousal. Use the focused breathing technique if appropriate.

BLAST OFF!

PERSONAL PRE-COMPETITION PLAN

Competition:

Venue:

Date/Time:

10

9

8

7

6

5

4

3

2

1

BLAST OFF!

No matter what your sport, detailed competition preparation sets the scene for successful performance

So, start using your notebook now and devise your own pre-ferred structure for recording your routines. If this starts with just a list of the critical elements on which you need to focus at each stage of the preparation process, then that is a good start. You'll find that you get better at planning, and implementing, competition routines the more you practise them. So, give them a chance and don't be too hasty in changing them if you're not entirely comfortable immediately. Like all aspects of mental skills training, there are no magic wands and no miracles to be experienced overnight!

Key elements in competition planning

Whichever form your competition routines end up taking, at the very least they should include attention to the seven criti-cal elements identified below. Without the inclusion of these basic elements, an athlete is gambling on the chance of attain-ing the ideal performance state — and if they do, it will prob-ably be a case of 'more luck than judgment'. So, as we ex-plained earlier, a professional approach is about making things happen and planning for success. It is not about keep-ing fingers crossed and hoping it will be all right on the day!

● 1. *Wake up with a positive state of mind*

Athletes should develop a routine to follow on the morning of a competition which will put themselves in a positive frame of mind. This may begin by thinking something really positive even before opening the eyes. *"I am prepared for today — I feel great"* sets the tone for the rest of the day and establishes a confident mood right from the start.

● 2. *Equipment check*

This is a critical element of any routine. Personal equipment should be checked and set out so that there are no frantic searches needed on the morning of competition. Many athletes make a list on a small card of all the equipment and personal clothing they wish to have at the competition. The card is then taped to the inside of their equipment bag so that each item can be checked off as it is put in.

● 3. *Baseline arousal check*

Athletes should begin preparation for each competition at the same level of arousal. This may involve several arousal checks. But it is vital that the timing of these checks is appropriate and enough time is allowed for the implementation of techniques to alter arousal if necessary.

● 4. *Confidence check*

Athletes should check their level of confidence in the same way they check their level of arousal. A well-rehearsed list of personal positive affirmations should be available for use as, and when, necessary.

● 5. *Mental rehearsal*

A specific time should be established when the athlete will mentally rehearse performance. Many athletes find the period between warm-up and competition a good time for this activity.

● 6. *Meals*

Meals should be scheduled so that time is provided for obtaining the proper foods and so that eating is not rushed.

● 7. *Physical warm-up*

A physical warm-up routine must be very well practised during training and must be an absolute priority on competition day. Too many athletes attempt to fit physical warm-up in, and around, everything else which is taking place and end up not devoting enough time and attention on carrying their routine out properly. The psychological effects of a consistent physical warm-up should not be underestimated.

Planning for "what ifs?"

We have explained earlier in the book that sport competition rarely runs smoothly. The lead up to competition is equally subject to disruption and therefore it is essential that an athlete's competition preparation is flexible enough to cope with last minute problems and changes. Indeed, the professional athlete is the one who can deal with changes to routine in a calm and confident manner. One of the best ways to prepare for these types of disruption is to use "what if?" scenarios (see sample list below). In other words, spend time considering, and discussing, how you would cope if something significantly disruptive occurred at a critical time.

Sample list of "what if?" situations

What if ...

— *a boot lace or clip breaks 10 minutes before the start of competition?*

— *the bus breaks down and you arrive at the competition venue 15 minutes before the start when you usually like 90 minutes?*

— *5 minutes before the start of competition you realise that you're too nervous?*

— *your coach uncharacteristically shouts at you as you're warming up?*

— *your favourite changing position is taken by another athlete?*

— *you feel an old muscle injury twinge during the latter stages of your warm-up?*

— *immediately prior to the start of competition, you are informed that a national selector has travelled from London to watch you play?*

— *the night before competition you learn that you will be opposite the same player who marked you out of the game last season?*

— *during your warm-up you cannot seem to get a personal problem out of your mind?*

"WHAT IF?" PLANNER

Identify possible "what if?" situations which may occur relating to a competition and then consider appropriate coping strategies

Competition:

Venue:

Date/Time:

What if?	Action:
1.	
2.	
3.	
4.	

The acronym 'PRO' is a useful reminder cue in these, and other, 'what if' situations:-

P — professional
R — reactions and actions
O — only.

Consider how the ultimate professional athlete would react in these situations as a guide to your own appropriate responses.

When all is said and done the Olympic Games are all about risk management. The athletes are going to compete in a jungle and I have to help prepare them for that. To me it's mental. Can they cope? Can they reproduce the form? Who has got the bottle? Unfortunately, you cannot predict who will be the victim and who will be the victor. I have to assess the risks and then manage them for the athletes. I do this by thorough preparation. I try to imagine every possible contingency.

Craig Hilliard, Australian Track & Field Coach

I began..to visualise different problematical situations that might arise in reality, and would have to be dealt with. I found that if I could anticipate them, they did not seem to be so bad... I went through every situation that could possibly arise, then imagined the best way of dealing with it... I try to imagine the stadium itself, what it will smell and sound like, what I will see, what it might feel like to be there. If I think anything might be about to happen, no matter how small or large, I focus on it in advance, and by anticipating it I learn to deal with it.

Sally Gunnell, discussing race preparation in the 1992 Olympics

Dealing with the media

To conclude this chapter, we shall briefly review the issue of dealing with the media. As athletes become more successful, they eventually become the focus of some sort of media attention. This attention usually begins at the local level. Professional competition preparation therefore involves competent handling of the media which actually consists of two angles. First, promoting yourself, the team and the sport in an active way. And second, being able to confidently deal with the media when they approach you.

Certain basic skills can be useful in either of these two situations. We have set these out in point form below on the basis of work we have done in the past with a media consultant.

● *Taking the initiative*

1.   Target local media first. Start small and build up.

2.   Find out the name of the sports editors.

3.   Provide them with a list of key competitions and events over the forthcoming 18 months or so.

4.   Prepare a biography of yourself on one sheet of paper.

     Full name.

     Date and place of birth.

     Current place of residence (i.e., town).

     Basic guide to your sport (i.e., creative midfield player).

     Your club.

     Years in representative squad and perhaps one or two statistics (e.g., scored a hat trick against Newtown in 1995).

     A contact telephone or FAX number for you.

5.   Decide on some key messages about yourself, your club, the representative squad which you would like to see communicated in the media.

6.   Phone the sports editor to make initial contact — a good time to do this is about a week before a key event.

Don't be disheartened if the response is lukewarm — this is common. Try to build a relationship step by step — this will be facilitated if you prove to be reliable in supplying information and particularly if you can think of some sort of "newsworthy angle". BUT, only make contact when it is important — don't swamp them!

7.   Remember the "five Ws" when submitting material for the media:

WHO: is involved?

WHAT: is it about?

WHERE: did it take place?

WHEN: did it take place?

WHY: is this interesting?

8.   Help to teach yourself what is newsworthy by reading other sports reports and watching TV sports news coverage — it's not always scandal that makes the news!

9.   If possible, try to preview an event with a call two or three days in advance of the editor's deadlines. You'll need to find out which day of the week your local paper is produced or the best time of day to reach your contact.

10. Always be reliable. Journalists are very busy and work to tight schedules. If you prove to be unreliable they will give up on you extremely quickly.

11. Success in gaining coverage is often sporadic. Be patient and persevere.

12. Remember to keep copies of newspaper reports or radio/TV clips. These are essential in building up a portfolio which is absolutely crucial in the quest for sponsorship. Don't be too modest. If the journalists and sponsors don't come to you then you must go to them!

● *How to prepare a press release*

1. Keep it concise. Never more than one sheet of A4 for the "story" (you can add team lists and statistics on separate sheets if relevant).

2. Make your paragraphs short and type (or write) in at least 1.5 line spacing. (Editors like to write amendments between lines).

3. Put the "news" in the first paragraph (and your sponsor's name). (Editors will cut the story from the bottom upwards).

4. Make sure the "5 Ws" appear in the first paragraph.

5. Clearly mark your sheet as a Press Release and indicate when the news is available for use — preferably "for immediate use".

6. ALWAYS put a contact name and number at the foot of the release (and make sure that person is available to answer calls).

7. Try and make sure that your release title is eye-catching.

8. If possible, add a quotation from yourself or a coach.

9. Remember, the media will always want to know people's ages, occupations, place of residence and full names.

10. Decide on a "house style" for names and stick to it (e.g., Freda Bloggs — followed by Freda for each subsequent mention, or Mrs. Freda Bloggs — followed by Mrs. Bloggs).

● *Dealing with interviews*

1. Find out who the journalists are and who they represent.

2. Find out what sort of questions they are going to ask, so that:

    (i)   you can say "no comment" before it all starts;

    (ii) you can direct them to someone else who may be more appropriate;

    (iii) you have a little time to prepare some slick answers.

3. Try to work in your key messages and facts to your answers.

4. Try to make your sentences short and snappy. If you don't speak in sound bites, they will edit and they may not edit in the way you like.

5. If a photographer or film crew is present consider the backdrop in terms of the image it conveys.

6. Be assertive when necessary — if they want to interview you while you're preparing for competition then say no if you feel it would have an adverse effect on your performance.

7. Remember, unless the interview is live, you can always ask to do re-takes. Don't be embarrassed about this request — it happens all the time.

8. For TV interviews:

    (i) assume a comfortable position and stick to it;

    (ii) look at the interviewer (not the camera);

    (iii) keep your body straight — when you're nervous there is a tendency to either back away or lean inwards;

    (iv) relax and treat the interviewer as a "normal person";

    (v) avoid using nicknames or jargon — this turns the average viewer off usually.

If you are interested in professional advice on press releases and dealing with the media, contact Caroline Searle (on whose advice this section of the chapter is based) at the address below.

Matchtight Media,
PO Box 9,
Torpoint,
Cornwall, PL11 2YH.
Tel: 01752-823226

Or, of course, ask a friendly journalist or sports editor locally.

The competition preparation fundaMENTALs

- *1. Approach competition, training and other aspects of lifestyle in a professional manner.*

- *2. Use a personalised training review chart to monitor the quality of your mental and physical preparation for competition.*

- *3. Develop organised routines for each of the different phases of the competition period. Practise these routines regularly.*

- *4. Identify a variety of "what if?" situations which may occur in your sport and consider strategies for coping with the potential disruption to an ideal performance state.*

- *5. Devise a media plan for preparing press releases as well as dealing with requests for interviews.*

Chapter 10
Putting it all together: The final game plan

If you have worked hard enough to render yourself worthy of going to Olympia, if you have not been idle or ill-disciplined, then go with confidence; but those who have not trained in this fashion, go where they will.

Philostratus, Greek philosopher

Your "Mental Game Plan"

When considering your newly developed "mental game plan" (MGP), perhaps the most important point to remember is that you will need to be very committed to regularly practising your programme. Sport psychologists recommend that if mental training is to have an effect, you need to practise systematically. Typically, mental training plans will require you to carry out several sessions of mental training each week. Try to think of your MGP as you would a physical training plan. If you want to maintain the condition of a muscle, it requires regular training. If the training stops, the muscle loses condition. Exactly the same principle applies for the training of your mind. Practise regularly, and your mind will be well

185

> Positive psychology is so powerful in enhancing performance... Before the Olympics I put in as many hours doing ... mental training, including reading books and thinking about how I was going to perform as I did in everything else combined, range training, aerobic training, stretching, and weight training.
>
> *Linda Thom*, *1984 Olympic shooting Gold Medalist*

> Weight training and fitness is the easy bit. It's the mental stuff which is the real challenge.
>
> *Ron Richards*, *Canadian 3 time Olympian ski jumper*

prepared for competition. Let the training slip, and the effects of the previous training will soon wear off. The requirements aren't great, so with a lot of conviction and belief in your programme the training should become second nature to you.

Although it may seem a simple task to stick to your MGP, you should not assume that this training will become an integral part of your overall preparation routine overnight. Experiences with other athletes tell us that even though there is a very high degree of acceptance of the usefulness of mental training, attempts to implement programmes are not always successful. Athletes often find that within only a few weeks of beginning a programme of mental training the regularity of the training drops off. This is seldom due to a belief that the training is not worthwhile, but is caused more through poor time-management and lack of prioritisation of the mental training. Obviously, the more steps you can take to help stop this drop-off, the more benefit you will stand to gain from your MGP.

As with any form of training, there is often a degree of monotony to mental training. However, by following a few

"**Although you can train your body physically by sheer persistence, it's much harder to train your mind... All this visualisation did not come to me in a flash. I had to work at it, and learn how to use it.**"

Sally Gunnell, *Olympic Gold Medalist*
and World Champion hurdler

simple rules in the early stages of your programme you can lay the foundations for successful mental training which will readily become an accepted part of your standard training sessions, and preparation for competition.

As there is a potential problem with sticking to the training, the aim of this chapter is to outline techniques and approaches to mental training which will assist you with the successful implementation and long-term adherence to your MGP.

Sticking with mental training

Arising from our work with hundreds of athletes from many different sports in both the United Kingdom and North America, it has become apparent to us that it is not always enough to simply teach athletes the relevant mental skills to help with getting psyched for competition. More often than not, there is a need to assist athletes with the actual integration of the new programme into existing training routines. Through careful consideration of such factors as when to carry out mental training sessions, how long the sessions should be, and how frequently the athlete needs to use the sessions, it is possible to increase the likelihood that athletes will stick with the programme requirements. It will only be through good adherence to your plan that mental training will become an accepted part of your preparation for competition. As we have said, your aim should be to approach your mental training just as you would approach other aspects of your performance preparation, such as the physical and technical components of training. If the difference between winning and losing comes down to who is most prepared on the day, then equal importance should be given to both mental and physical preparation. A car cannot function efficiently unless all the different systems are working together, in harmony. Similarly, all systems within you need to be in perfect working order to produce a top performance, and this will only be achieved by making sure that everything, mind and body, has been fully prepared. Keep this in mind all the time when you are doing your mental training.

Top tips for MGP adherence

● *1 Personalise your MGP*

Perhaps the most crucial aspect for ensuring adherence to mental training programmes is the individual tailoring of both programme content and scheduling of sessions. This means that you must be completely sure that the focus of your programme is absolutely right for you. You will need to identify a programme content that meets your requirements, and is also comprised of content with which you can associate. Therefore, from the relevant chapters in this book, develop a programme content that is meaningful to you, and you feel will be of benefit to you. There are examples of introductory sessions for you to use within the other chapters of this book, but as much as possible we would recommend that you remodel these examples to match your own specific needs. Look to make these changes as soon as you feel you have developed the fundamental skills sufficiently. Take the concepts that you read and adapt the ideas so that the content is relevant to you and your sport.

Probably the best way to make sure your MGP is most appropriately designed to meet your performance needs is to use the Performance Profiling process outlined in chapter 2. By going through the process that we have described, it will be very apparent to you which aspects of performance you need to build your MGP around. Look at the mental elements of the profile where there is the greatest discrepancy between your ideal and current scores, and use this as the foundation for your MGP. For example, if you have identified confidence and remaining calm as essential performance qualities, and there is a high discrepancy score on each of these qualities, then your MGP should be designed to improve confidence and arousal regulation. Using this problem-solving approach should ensure that you have an MGP that you will feel is worthy time investment. Getting this aspect of your MGP right from the very beginning of your training is very important to the long-term effectiveness of your programme.

● *2 Establish how important MGP is to you*

Early on, even before finishing reading this book, you should decide just how important mental training is to helping you achieve your sporting goals.

Our research tells us that athletes who really believe that mental training will help them fulfil their potential are the ones who find it easiest to adhere to their training. No great surprises there. This may seem like stating that birds can fly, but the important thing to note is that most athletes believe that mental preparation can benefit them However, only a few ever successfully establish an MGP.

If you want your mental training to be successful, you really must commit yourself to it, from this point onwards. If you put the effort in, you will certainly reap the rewards.

Performance analysis

Carry out this short exercise to help establish how important mental preparation could be to you.

1.   Think of your competitions in terms of mental, physical, and technical requirements. Identify the percentage contribution of each of these aspects to producing a peak performance.

2.   Now identify the percentage of time you devote to each of these aspects in training.

3.   Compare the percentages to see how appropriately you are spending your training time in relation to your competitive needs.

We find that with most athletes they identify that the mental side of performance plays a very important role in producing a peak performance. However, when analysing their training very little time at all is devoted to this aspect of performance preparation. It makes sense to balance your preparation time in order that each aspect of performance is given the necessary amount of preparation.

● 3 *Establish an appropriate structure to your MGP*

We have suggested that athletes often fail to stick with their mental training because of poor time management, or lack of prioritisation of mental preparation. If you have decided that mental training is something you seriously want to use, then through some simple time-planning strategies you can maximise the likelihood of gaining performance related benefits.

One useful approach is to identify time during the week which will be your mental training times. This is a typical approach that you would use with other training, so employ it with the mental training too. Having established these times your mental training then has a priority time which nothing else can interfere with.

A simple process which will help give you a mental training structure is described below.

Procedure for structuring mental training

1. Write out a typical week's timetable and identify all your existing commitments (e.g., work, training, family time, competition times, etc.).

2. Now identify 'spare' time periods in your week when you would be free to carry out mental training (e.g., travelling on public transport, showering/bathing, equipment maintenance, breaks in training sessions, etc.).

3. Write out how many times a week you want to carry out your mental training, and how long you expect each session to be.

4. Fit these sessions into the times highlighted in number 2, or use number 1 timetable to find a new time for mental training where you can be certain you will have no other time commitments.

5. Write out a new timetable, including your mental training commitments, and put this somewhere visible to act as a regular reminder of your new routine.

You can make use of this process on a regular basis by writing out a training plan for each week, in advance. Write out your target training in pencil, and at the end of the week complete the timetable in ink for those sessions you actually completed. This approach acts as a very simple goal-setting and review process and, as highlighted in chapter 2, it is often a good idea to have these goals in a visible place, so they can become more public, and family and friends can help remind you of your targets and check that you are achieving them. This approach might be one you want to take with your other forms of training as well.

When you are looking for appropriate times to schedule your mental training there are several things you should consider. First, schedule times when you know you are not going to be disturbed. Athletes quite often find that if they don't plan appropriately their sessions get interrupted frequently. Try to avoid this by using times when other people are not around, using a time when you know you will be able to find a quiet place, or by letting likely distracters know when you will be doing your mental training.

A second thing to keep in mind when scheduling your sessions is to identify times which you can always use, even if your routine changes. We have found in the past that if an athlete's usual daily routine gets interrupted (e.g., they travel to a competition or training camp, visit a relative, etc.) then they will quite often forget to do their mental training. If you schedule your mental training in conjunction with behaviours which you will carry out wherever you are, or however much your routine changes, then you will be more likely to keep the training going. For example, you may wish to build your mental training into a wake-up routine on a daily basis. It is likely that you will still be physically training even when your routine gets disrupted, so building your mental training sessions into the warm-up or warm-down phases of your physical training sessions is often a good idea for adherence purposes, as well as being a good way to prepare for, or review, your training.

Don't forget that if you change the focus, content and duration of your training you may need to reschedule your mental training timetable.

● 4 *Use a mental training diary to record your progress*

Many athletes with whom we have worked have found it useful to record their mental training in a diary. Not only is this a good way of seeing exactly how much you have achieved during a specific period of time, but it can also be a good way of assessing how well your mental training skills are developing. We have found that by using a 1-10 quality rating scale (1 = poor, 10 = excellent) for each session athletes can get a good idea of whether or not their skills are improving. It can often be very motivating to review your diary entries and see your ratings slowly increasing. If the scores are not on the up, then you will be able to identify when it might be the appropriate time to tweak your training a bit.

Furthermore, by recording their feelings before, during and after a session, athletes start getting a good idea of what helps improve the quality of a mental training session. For instance, when studying diary entries athletes can see whether their training is of greater quality before or after physical training. We have found that some athletes prefer to use mental training in the mornings as this helps to improve the quality of the sessions. You may be able to tailor your MGP more specifically to your preferred training times and styles if you record every session in a diary.

Some athletes find that by keeping the diary in a prominent place (e.g., by their bedside or on the fridge door) it acts as a constant reminder to actually stick with the MGP.

So, make yourself up a simple training diary such as the one on the following page, and try recording your sessions to see if it helps with your programme. In order to provide you with useful information we usually include the following in an athlete mental training diary:

- Date
- Time of day session carried out
- Duration of session
- Content of session
- General comments about the session
- Quality rating on 1-10 scale.

MENTAL GAME PLAN DIARY

DAY	TIME	DATE	SESSION	DURATION	COMMENTS	QUALITY
Monday						
Tuesday						
Wednesday						
Thursday						
Friday						
Saturday						
Sunday						

● 5 Integrate mental and physical training

Perhaps one of the most useful ways of helping you to stick with your MGP is to recommend that you combine your mental and physical training as soon as possible. It is likely that in the first place you will need to carry out the majority of your mental training sessions in isolation from the external distractions that are typically present at a training venue. However, once you have got used to the techniques, and feel you are regularly producing quality sessions, start to use your mental training during your actual physical training time. The main reason for recommending this is that we have found that athletes often perceive their physical and mental training to be completely separate aspects of performance preparation. Therefore, it is often the case that if an athlete feels they need to devote extra time to physical or technical preparation the mental training has to make way. If you combine the different modes of training, then this casting-off of your MGP is less likely to happen. Furthermore, it is obvious that during competition we rely on mental, physical and technical aspects of performance to work "in sync". Therefore, if you regularly practise all these components of performance as one you will be getting a much fuller preparation for the demands of competition.

A good example of how to combine the different aspects of performance preparation comes from downhill ski racers. During weight training sessions there are natural recovery periods between sets of exercise repetitions. In these recovery times some racers carry out imagery sessions in which they imagine themselves skiing a particular course such as the Val d'Isere run. They actually crouch down into a tucked position with arms forward to physically simulate the racing position during the imagery.

As well as using these rest periods effectively, as has previously been suggested, you may wish to build mental training sessions into your training time before you start to train (in order to get focused on the session ahead), or in order to review and appraise the session you have just done. As well as helping to improve the particular mental skill you are using, the preview or review session should act to enhance the quality of your other aspects of training.

So, we recommend that you identify key times during your typical training sessions where you might be able to carry out your mental training sessions, or use mental training to enhance the quality of your other forms of preparation.

● 6   *Update and review your MGP regularly*

As mentioned at the beginning of this chapter, boredom with programmes can often lead to athletes stopping using them. The best way of avoiding this problem is to prevent yourself becoming bored in the first place. We have found that by a simple process of regularly updating an MGP this problem is usually solved. If the focus of your programme needs to re-main the same then this updating needs a certain amount of imagination, but within the chapters of this book you should get a pretty good idea of the many ways in which you can achieve the same mental training objective. We would recom-mend that you look to alter your programme every 6-8 weeks. This does not mean a major re-working of all the elements, simply alter some of the things you are doing. For example, if you are focusing on building confidence, you have the choice of using imagery (replaying best ever performances, imagin-ing yourself performing to the best of your ability, imagining beating a tough opponent, etc.), reviewing highlight videos, and using confidence building statements, to name but a few approaches.

As well as changing the content of your MGP it is also possible that from time to time you will need to change the fo-cus of your MGP. Through the regular use of the Performance Profiling technique, as recommended in chapter 2, you will easily identify when it is time to change the focus of your MGP. Similarly if you regularly use the Mental Skills Ques-tionnaire described in chapter 2, you will also be able to deter-mine whether or not you need a new programme focus. Again, you may want to carry this process out every 6-8 weeks to help you keep your programme moving forward.

The mental training fundaMENTALs

● *1.* *Use Performance Profiling to help you identify the direction that your MGP should be taking. By identifying your strengths and weaknesses, you can build up an MGP that you feel will be a worthwhile investment of your time.*

● *2.* *Personalise your programme as early as possible. Make sure that the sessions you use contain images, words, sounds, situations, etc., which are meaningful to you.*

● *3.* *Integrate your physical and mental training routines as early as possible. Do this by scheduling mental training sessions either immediately before, or immediately after, your physical training. Once you feel ready, use your mental training during your physical training sessions. In this way, you can use the physical training to improve the quality of your mental training, and vice versa.*

● *4.* *Build up your programme slowly. Start with a 'little and often' approach to mental training, as this will help you get used to the requirements of the training.*

● *5.* *Plan ahead when you are going to do your mental training sessions for each week. Be sure to find times when you know the mental training will be your only focus.*

● 6.   Plan the content of each session in detail. Review each session to help with progress evaluation.

● 7.   Don't be afraid to experiment with the techniques that have been outlined. Follow the general guidelines to begin with, but bring in your own ideas to help improve the quality of the sessions you carry out.

● 8.   Use chapter 2 to help you plan out your mental training goals, and how you will go about achieving them.

● 9.   Build in a variety of sessions to your programme that are designed to achieve the same goal, and update your programme regularly (every 6-8 weeks). In this way you should limit boredom with the programme, and you will always have something new to aim for.

● 10. Concentrate hard for the first two to three months of your MGP on carrying out your training on a regular basis. If you can get into a set routine over this period of time, it should lay the foundations for long-term use of mental training.

● 11. Recruit the help of others close to you (e.g., coach, team-mates, family). Through them either joining in with your mental training, reminding you of when it should be done, or simply taking an interest in what you are doing you can gain valuable support during times when you might let the training slip.

So there it is. You should now have your Mental Game Plan. With commitment and regular practice, you will be well-placed to reach new levels of performance and consistency. As we stated at the end of chapter 1, performance under pressure can be up to 30% better or 30% worse. You should now know why this is so and realise that you CAN take control and achieve performance excellence. Remember the ABC of mental training to get the most out of your Mental Game Plan:

A*pply the various skills to your own needs and sporting requirements.*

B*elieve in yourself and your Mental Game Plan at all times.*

C*ommit yourself fully to making mental training an important part of your performance preparation.*

Use your MGP to achieve performance excellence!

Appendix:
Where to go now

Coaching courses in sport psychology

The National Coaching Foundation runs a variety of courses in sport psychology and mental training. These courses are pitched at different levels and are useful for performers as well as coaches. If you wish to find out more about these courses and where they run, we suggest you contact the NCF head office at the following address:

> The National Coaching Foundation
> 114 Cardigan Road, Headingley, LEEDS, LS6 3BJ   (UK)
> Tel: 0113 274 4802   FAX: 0113 275 5019

Using a sport psychologist

The authors of this book act in an advisory capacity to a wide range of individuals and organisations. They run workshops for clubs and teams as well as providing specialist assistance in the form of one-to-one consultancy. If you wish to discuss the possibility of working with them, they can be contacted at the address below:

> Sports Dynamics, 88 Baldwin Avenue
> EASTBOURNE,   BN21 1UP (UK)
> Tel/FAX: 01323 723 603

Alternatively, you can seek the advice of a sport psychologist in your local area but it is recommended that you use individuals who are suitably qualified and experienced in the delivery of sport psychology services — i.e., someone who has official credentials.

Two accreditation schemes for sport psychologists currently exist in the UK. One is administered by the British Association of Sport and Exercise Sciences. The other by the British Olympic Association. The contact details of each are provided below:

Chair of Psychology Section
British Association of Sport
     and Exercise Sciences
114 Cardigan Road, Headingley
LEEDS   LS6 3BJ (UK)
Tel: 0113 230 7558
FAX: 0113 275 5019

Chair of Psychology
     Advisory Group
British Olympic Association
1, Wandsworth Plain
LONDON   SW18 1EH (UK)
Tel: 0181 871 2677
FAX: 0181 871 9104

Acknowledgements

The authors wish to thank the following individuals and organisations for their respective contributions to the production of this book.

Photographs
Richard Cobbing — *taken by Mark Junak and courtesy of the British Ski Federation.*
Graham Bell — *taken by Mike Hewitt and courtesy of the British Ski Federation.*
Karen Smithies — *courtesy of Karen Smithies.*
All other photographs were provided by the Sportsphoto Agency Photographic Library, 20 Clifton Street, Scarborough, YO12 7SR. Tel: 01723 367264. Fax: 01723 500117.

Line drawings
P.J. Bull.

Quotations
Rob Andrew (p.66, p.106, p.108, p.115, p.148, p.149 and p.166).
From: *Rob Andrew: A Game and a Half.* Published 1995 by Coronet Books. Reprinted with kind permission.

Kirsten Barnes (p. 11 and p.34).
From: "Sport Psychology: The Performer's Perspective". Invited lecture at the University of Brighton 1995.

Simon Barnes (p.1); Will Carling (p.19); Nicola Fairbrother (p.59 and p.115); Alan Lee (p.139); Michael Atherton (p.7); Nick Faldo (p.6); Jonathan Edwards (p.115).
From: *The Times* newspaper. Reprinted with kind permission.

Sylvie Bernier (p.3); Anne Ottenbrite (p.122); Bob Molle (p.166); Linda Thom (p.71 and p.186); Steve Podborski (p.69 and p.105); Jay Triano (p.70); Alex Bauman (p.68); Brian Orser (p.71); Alwyn Morris (p.72).
From: *Psyched: Inner Views of Winning* by T. Orlick & J. Partington. Copyright 1986 by Coaching Association of Canada. Reprinted with kind permission.

Sir Donald Bradman (p.85); Jean-Claude Killy (p.59); Martina Navratilova (p.10); Walter Hagen (p.111); Philostratus (p.185); Reggie Jackson (p.59); Vince Lombardi (p.158); Bjorn Borg (p.13).
From: *The Guinness Dictionary of Sports Quotations* by Colin Jarman. Published 1990 by Guinness Publishing. Reprinted with kind permission.

Jo Chamberlain (p.12); Barbara Daniels (p.141 and p.152); Karen Smithies (p.42); Clare Taylor (p.151); Richard Cobbing (p.131).
From: Personal communication with the authors.

Frank Dick (p.2); John Monie (p.5); Matt Biondi (p.115); Michael Johnson (p.115); Jack Nicklaus (p.72); Steve Backley (p.125); Ian Botham (p.128); Boris Becker (p.115); Gary Lineker (p.150); George Allen (p.165).
From: *The Sporting World* by D. Lynam and D. Teasdale. Published 1994 by BBC Books. Reprinted with kind permission.

Ray Floyd (p.16, p.65, p.94, p.115, and p.161).
From: *From 60 yards In* by R. Floyd. Published 1989 by Harper Perennial.
Reprinted with kind permission.

Doug Frobel (p.54); Ron Richards (p.186).
From: Panel discussion at the World Congress on Mental Training and
Excellence, Ottawa, 1995.

Shane Gould (p.116); Carl Lewis (p.141); Robert Clift (p.151); Mac Wilkins
(p.164); Craig Hilliard (p.179).
From: *Pressures and the Olympic Village*. Produced by The British Olympic
Association in 1995. Reprinted with kind permission.

Sally Gunnell (p.17, p.41, p.68. p.134. p.166, p.168, p.179, and p.187).
From: *Sally Gunnell: Running Tall*. Published 1994 by Bloomsbury Publishing.
Reprinted with kind permission.

Richard Hadlee (p.53 and p.74).
From: *At the Double* by Richard Hadlee with Tony Francis. Published 1985 by
Random Century Group. Reprinted with kind permission.

Vic Marks (p.110).
From: *The Observer* newspaper. Reprinted with kind permission.

Terence O'Rorke (p.8).
From: *Mansell, Formula One and Indycar Champion* by T. O'Rorke. Copyright
1992 Grenville Books. Reprinted with kind permission.

Darrell Pace (p.100).
From: "On target with mental skills: An interview with Darrell Pace" by R.S.
Vealey and S.M. Walter, *The Sport Psychologist*, (Vol. 8, No.4), p. 431. Copyright
1994 by Human Kinetics Publishers. Reprinted with kind permission.

Kate Pace (p.115).
From: "The Essence of Excellence: A Personal Perspective", Keynote lecture at
the World Congress on Mental Training and Excellence, Ottawa, 1995.

John Roberts (p.iii).
From: *The Independent* newspaper. Reprinted with kind permission.

Robin Smith (p.107).
From: *Quest for Number One* by Robin Smith and John Crace. Published 1993 by
Boxtree. Reprinted with kind permission.

Jackie Stewart (p.157).
From: *Jackie Stewart's Principles of Performance Driving* Edited by Alan Henry.
Published 1992 Hazleton Publishing. Reprinted with kind permission.

Teddy Sheringham (p.142).
From: *The Daily Telegraph* newspaper. Reprinted with kind permission.

The Mental Training Questionnaire

Appreciation is extended to Professor Lew Hardy and Dave Nelson for grant-
ing permission to adapt their Sport-related Psychological Skills Questionnaire.

Index

205